VOLPONE, OR THE FOX

BY

BEN JONSON

EDITED

WITH AN INTRODUCTION AND NOTES

BY

J. B. BAMBOROUGH, M.A.

MACMILLAN

First Edition 1963
Reprinted 1967 (twice), 1969, 1970, 1974

Published by
MACMILLAN EDUCATION LTD
London and Basingstoke
Associated companies and representatives
throughout the world

SBN 333 010361

Printed in Great Britain by
ROBERT MACLEHOSE AND CO LTD
The University Press, Glasgow

List of Contents

v

Acknowledgments

THE editor and publishers wish to acknowledge their indebtedness to the following, who have kindly given permission for the use of copyright material: Mr. T. S. Eliot, O.M., and Messrs. Faber & Faber, Ltd., for the extracts from *Selected Essays*, and the Oxford University Press, for the modernized text of *Volpone*, from *Five Plays*, by Ben Jonson, in *The World's Classics*.

Introduction

NOBODY knows exactly when or where Ben Jonson was born, but it was probably in 1572 and in London. His father, who was a clergyman, died before Ben was born, and his mother married again; her second husband is described as 'a bricklayer', but he was probably rather more what we would call a 'jobbing builder', and seems to have been quite successful. The family lived near Trafalgar Square, and all his life Jonson never moved far from the centre of London. He went to Westminster School, where he was taught by the famous scholar and antiquary William Camden, but he seems never to have attended a university, or at the most only for a very short time. Probably his family was too poor to send him to Oxford or Cambridge and instead he was apprenticed when he left school to his stepfather's trade. Disliking bricklaying, he enlisted as a soldier and served in the English Expeditionary Force in the Netherlands. Apart from this, very little is known of his early life until he began to become known, about 1597, as a dramatist. He may have started in the theatre as an actor — tradition says not a very good one. He had his first big success in 1598 with *Every Man in his Humour*, which was performed by Shakespeare's company with Shakespeare in the cast, and in 1599 he followed it up with *Every Man out of his Humour*.

In these two plays Jonson was trying to 'regularize' English stage comedy — that is, to bring it more in accordance with the 'rules' of drama which Renaissance critics had evolved from their study of the Ancients. Jonson had a very tidy and well-organized mind and a strong sense of fact, and as he says in many places (including the Preface to *Volpone*) he could not bear the incompetent construction and slipshod writing of much Elizabethan drama, nor its 'romantic' improbabilities and absurdities. His own strength lay in the realistic portrayal of contemporary life and manners, though he could also, when he wished, be fanciful and extravagant. He kept this side of his imagination, however, for his masques, and his comedies never stray far from commonsense and the everyday, or, as he put it himself,

... deeds and language such as men do use,
And persons such as *Comedy* would choose
When she would show an image of the times. ...

An 'image of the times' is exactly what Jonson provides. Nearly all his comedies are set in contemporary London — *Volpone* is one of the few exceptions — and from them we can gain an extraordinarily vivid impression of Jacobean life, especially of its oddities and eccentricities. A concentration on oddity and eccentricity is the essence of the 'Comedy of Humours', of which Jonson was virtually the inventor. The nature of the Comedy of Humours has often been misunderstood. The 'humours' belong to the world of Renaissance psychological theory, according to which a man's 'temperament' or disposition was the result of the balance of the four humours in the blood. If a man had a predominance of the humour of phlegm he would be of a phlegmatic disposition, or if it were choler that dominated he would be choleric; the other two possible temperaments were the sanguine, in which blood predominated, and the melancholic, produced by an excess of black bile. In loose parlance, however, 'to have a humour' meant very much the same as 'to have a complex about something' means today: a man might say that 'it was his humour' to hate cats, for example, or even to wear a particular sort of hat. Jonson objected to this slang use of the term, and even more to the kind of affectation to which it was applied. In the Introduction to *Every Man out of his Humour* he defines 'Humour' as he thinks it ought to be used, and he then goes on to say that he will 'scourge' the kind of person who uses it to describe his own stupid ways of behaving. He does not, as is sometimes said, say that he is going to write only about characters who are examples of 'humour' in the strict sense, and indeed if he had done so he would have had a cast of only four characters. What he does do is to satirize all kinds of behaviour which seem to him deviations from the norm of reasonable and moral conduct; sometimes these are serious deviations, as they are in *Volpone*: more often they are comparatively trivial.

In the last years of the sixteenth century there was a marked taste for satire of all kinds, and Jonson's type of comedy suited this taste very well. He was, however, very outspoken, particularly about other writers, and personally he was a rather aggressive and quarrelsome man (in 1598 he was arrested and might have hanged for killing another actor in a duel). His first 'Humour' plays made him famous, but they also made him enemies.

His next play, *Cynthia's Revels* (1600), was written for performance at Court, but since much of it was a satirical attack on the stupidities of Court life it was not very well received. Jonson found himself the object of attack by other writers, notably Marston and Dekker. He attempted to silence his critics in *Poetaster* (1601) — in which, among other things, Marston is given an emetic to make him bring up all the obscure words in his vocabulary, and he and Dekker are forced to apologize to Jonson — but this did not put an end to the attacks, and for the time being Jonson gave up comedy and devoted himself to writing *Sejanus*, his first 'regular' tragedy, which appeared in 1603.

Sejanus was not a success. It is a very serious, carefully written and scholarly play; Jonson studied the Roman historians and tried to give as accurate a picture as he could of Roman life and customs. Unfortunately *Sejanus* is also rather a dull play, and it was hissed off the stage at its first performance. Jonson must have been very disappointed, but he received some consolation in the following year, when he was asked to write a masque for performance before King James as part of the Court festivities in the Christmas season of 1604–5. The masque was a kind of drama peculiar to the Courts of Renaissance noblemen and princes. Essentially it was a visit by 'strangers' — actually members of the Court in disguise — who came to pay their respects to the Prince, and to dance with the ladies and gentlemen of his Court, but around this central act there grew up an entertainment that had in it elements not only of drama but of ballet and opera as well. It was a very lavish and expensive form of entertainment, and a great deal of money was spent on costumes and scenery, and for this reason not many masques were performed at the Court of Queen Elizabeth, who was not given to wasting money. James was more extravagant and had a stronger sense of the sort of display expected of a Renaissance monarch, and he had at least one masque performed before him each year until the end of his reign — most of them written by Jonson. The writer's part in a masque was not in fact of prime importance, since the real emphasis was on the spectacle and the dancing, but Jonson would never admit this, and as a result frequently quarrelled with the producer. What his masques did do for Jonson, however, was to make him very well known at Court, and to provide him with a better source of income than writing for the stage. He did not abandon the theatre at once; in fact the next few years saw the production of his best comedies — *Volpone* late in 1605 or early in 1606, again acted by Shakespeare's company in London, and afterwards at Oxford and Cambridge; *Epicoene* in 1609, *The Alchemist* in 1610 and *Bartholomew Fair* in 1614. His only failure in this period was his second tragedy, *Catiline* (1611), which like *Sejanus* was too scholarly and slow-moving for the popular audience. Jonson never tried tragedy again. The ill-success of *Catiline* is much more than made up for by the four great comedies; they are the finest things he ever wrote, and all of them are still being staged today with great success.

In 1616 Jonson published all his plays and poems together in a big folio volume which he called his 'Works'. It was an extraordinarily bold thing to do at a time when plays were not considered serious literature at all, and people made fun of him for doing it. 'Works' to a Jacobean meant collections of philosophical or theological treatises, not trivialities such as plays. In the end, however, Jonson carried his point and succeeded in raising the status of the dramatist, so that today it would never occur to us to think that a playwright was not to be taken seriously. (It is also probably true that if it had not been for the publication of Jonson's folio in 1616 we should not have had the Shakespeare folio of 1623.) In the same year as the folio Jonson brought out *The Devil is an Ass*, and then for nine years he gave up the public theatre altogether. In this period he was at his zenith as a Court poet and was regarded virtually as Poet Laureate, though he was never actually given the title. He gathered round him a group of young poets who were known as 'the sons of Ben'; Herrick is the best known of these. They used to meet in the 'Apollo' room of an inn called 'The Devil and St. Dunstan' near Temple Bar in the City, and the innkeeper, Simon Wadloe ('Simon the cellarer'), is referred to in some of Jonson's plays and poems. In these years, apart from his commissions for Court masques, Jonson was writing poetry, criticism and history, but little of this was ever published (some was destroyed in a fire at his house in 1623). Altogether, although from our point of view it was the least productive period in his life, it was probably in Jonson's eyes the most happy and successful.

The death of King James in 1625 brought this period of success to an end. Charles I never thought as highly of Jonson as his father had done and although he gave him a pension and commissioned one or two masques from him, Jonson's position at Court was never the same, and he had to go back to the public stage. His four last plays (*The Staple of News*, 1625, *The New Inn*, 1629, *The Magnetic Lady*, 1632, and *The Tale of a Tub*, 1633) have never been regarded as among his best — Dryden called them Jonson's 'dotages' — though all of them have some merit. They were generally unsuccessful on the stage, and for the last years of his life Jonson was in poverty and debt, and also in sickness; in 1629 he suffered a stroke, from which he appears never to have recovered properly. He continued to write, and parts of unfinished plays were found among his papers after his death, but by 1637, when he died, he was almost forgotten. His friends published a volume of poems to his memory, but they failed to raise enough money to provide him with a tombstone in Westminster Abbey; eventually someone gave a workman eighteen pence to carve on the marble slab above his grave the famous epitaph, 'O RARE BEN JONSON'.

Until the end of the seventeenth century Jonson was regarded by many as the greatest English dramatist, superior to Shakespeare, and even Dryden could seriously debate their respective merits. Dryden's verdict that he admired Jonson, but he loved Shakespeare, marks the shift in the balance of Jonson's reputation, and from the beginning of the eighteenth century onwards no one has ever doubted his inferiority to Shakespeare. His plays continued to be acted — Garrick scored one of his greatest successes in the part of Abel Drugger in *The Alchemist* — but the coming of Romanticism finally turned opinion against him. Coleridge admired his vigour and sense of construction, and others in the nineteenth century had an affection for him (Dickens, who has a lot in common with Jonson, liked to act Bobadil in amateur productions of *Every Man in his Humour*), but his coarseness and his apparent lack of sympathy with his characters did not suit Victorian taste. The reaction against Victorianism in this century has swung critical opinion more in his favour, but there is no hope that he will ever seriously rival Shakespeare again. This is in some ways unfair, since he is not simply inferior to Shakespeare: he is a different kind of artist altogether. Jonson was a highly self-conscious and controlled writer with a very rigorous sense of what he wanted to do, and no one has ever written his particular sort of comedy better. It is not quite comedy as we normally understand it in this country; from Chaucer onwards our comedy has been kinder and more sympathetic than it has been on the continent of Europe. Jonson really belongs to the European tradition, and it is really Molière rather than Shakespeare with whom we should compare him. In such a comparison he is not disgraced.

Volpone is Jonson's greatest play, as far as vigour and power of impact are concerned, and it is also, for some people, the most difficult of his plays to understand and like. When he set out to write it he was obviously faced with a difficulty. The plot all hangs on Volpone's deception of his 'suitors'; by pretending to be old and ill and on the point of death he gets presents from them. The difficulty was that the custom of making presents to someone in the hope of becoming his heir was not an English but a Roman practice, known as 'captatio'. Jonson could not, therefore, set the play in contemporary England, as he usually did; instead he had to place the action in Venice ('captatio' was not a Venetian custom either, for that matter, but Venice was sufficiently far away to make it credible). Having decided to do this, Jonson went to some pains to get the Venetian atmosphere right, though he brought in the three English people, Sir Politic and Lady Would-be and Peregrine the traveller, to enable him to hit at English follies as well. As a result *Volpone* has a strange, exotic quality, which is heightened by the curious and sinister household which Volpone maintains (some critics have said that Volpone still behaves more like an ancient Roman than a modern Italian). *Volpone* is an alien comedy in other ways. Jonson was always a harsh and severe satirist of human failings, but never more so than in this play. The suitors are completely amoral and depraved, and even inhuman in their greed; Jonson gives them the names of birds of prey ('Voltore' means 'vulture', and 'Corbaccio' and 'Corvino' both mean 'raven'; 'Volpone', of course, means 'fox' and 'Mosca' 'fly'). In *Volpone*, too, Jonson broke his own rule that comedy should deal with 'follies, not with crimes'; when Corvino tries to prostitute his wife or Corbaccio testifies against his son they are guilty of something far worse than folly. As a result many have felt that *Volpone* cannot really be called a comedy at all, and some critics have preferred to regard it as a species of satirical tragedy. Jonson himself was aware that this view might be taken, and in his Dedication to the Universities of Oxford and Cambridge he apologizes for the harshness of the

punishments meted out at the end (comedies were supposed to
end happily, or at least on a light note), explaining that he made
the ending like this as a counter to those who complained that
contemporary dramatists were not careful enough to reward
virtue and punish vice.

The effect of *Volpone* is certainly unpleasant in some respects,
and it is true that the scene in which Volpone tries to rape Celia
is in tone and style more like what we expect from Elizabethan
tragedy — more similar, in fact, than anything in Jonson's own
tragedies. It is also true, as Coleridge pointed out, that anyone
but Jonson would have brought Celia and Bonario together at the
end, if only to send the audience away happier. Nevertheless we
are not justified in calling *Volpone* a tragedy, and still less in
thinking of Volpone himself as a tragic figure. He may be no
worse than the people around him, but equally he is not much
better; his only redeeming qualities are his cleverness and his
courage at the end. And in fact he is made as much of a fool as
anyone else in the play. He takes in the suitors, but he is taken in
himself by Mosca, and by trying to be too clever he puts himself
in the power of his own servant. For that matter even Mosca is
self-deceiving, for he does not realize that in the last result
Volpone, who is an aristocrat, will not allow himself to be tri-
umphed over by a parasite, even if it means accepting his own
punishment. Everyone in the play, except Peregrine and Sir
Politic (who has his own sort of folly), is dazzled by the thought
of wealth; even one of the judges is prepared to marry his
daughter to Mosca when he thinks that Mosca has inherited
Volpone's riches. Gold is their god; for gold they are prepared
to do anything, and blinded by gold they are incapable of seeing
the truth about anything. This is a vicious picture of society and
in many ways a true picture of the society of Jonson's own day, in
which large fortunes were being amassed by means as devious as
Volpone's own, but it is too limited a picture to be called tragic;
we have only to think for a moment of *King Lear* to see this.
Volpone must be thought of as a special sort of comedy in which
there are no 'good' characters, apart from the minor figures Celia
and Bonario (Peregrine is not wicked, but he is too heartless to be
sympathetic), and in which everyone is held up to ridicule. Its
nearest relatives are the comedies of Molière and the comedies of
the English Restoration, in which we are invited to laugh *at* the
characters rather than *with* them.

This sort of comedy was entirely in accordance with Renaissance critical theory, and *Volpone* is the best of its kind in English. It is very tightly constructed, and here the device of 'captatio' was useful, since so much of the action can be concentrated in one place, Volpone's bedroom. Jonson was always good at scenes of deception, and especially at deception which has to be improvised in a hurry, which is Mosca's speciality. Only in *The Alchemist* do we get such breath-taking quickness of thought and such skilful playing-off of one dupe against another, and only in *The Alchemist* is there the same mastery in the handling of technical jargon as in Volpone's mountebank speech. *Volpone* has also some of Jonson's finest dramatic verse. Just as he lacks Shakespeare's range of human sympathy, Jonson lacks Shakespeare's richness of metaphor and imagery, but his best poetry is always clear, precise, vigorous and powerful, and these qualities are exactly what this play requires. Volpone's opening speech sets the tone:

> Good morning to the day; and next my gold:
> Open the shrine, that I may see my saint.
> Hail the world's soul, and mine! More glad than is
> The teeming earth to see the long'd-for sun
> Peep through the horns of the celestial Ram,
> Am I, to view thy splendour darkening his. . . .

This has a kind of obsessed energy, an almost mad joy and excitement, while at the same time being quite precise and logical. Volpone really does live in a world in which gold is worshipped, and worshipped in language which blasphemously parodies the language of religion, and he really does believe that he who can get gold 'shall be noble, valiant, honest, wise' and have all the other virtues. The actor who plays Volpone has the opportunity to make us see and even for the moment accept an inverted scale of values in which riches are the supreme Good. Mosca has a similar speech at the beginning of Act III where he expresses his joy at being a successful parasite and intriguer, and we can feel in his lines the kind of movements he is making: he is literally dancing with pleasure. A quite different tone and movement comes in Celia's speech to Volpone:

> If you have ears that will be pierc'd: or eyes
> That can be open'd; a heart that may be touch'd;

> Or any part that yet sounds man about you:
> If you have touch of holy saints or heaven,
> Do me the grace to let me 'scape. . . .

This is an eloquent, anguished plea from a desperate girl, and it has a pathos which Jonson did not often achieve. The same scene has in Volpone's speeches a kind of horrible evocative beauty:

> A diamond would have bought Lollia Paulina
> When she came in like star-light, hid with jewels
> That were the spoils of provinces. . . ;

elsewhere in the play there are vivid images of squalor and degradation:

>   would you at once close
> Those filthy eyes of yours, that flow with slime,
> Like two frog-pits; and those same hanging cheeks,
> Cover'd with hide instead of skin. . . .

This is not poetry as we usually think of it, but it has the power and force of great writing.

In *Volpone*, as in all his works, Jonson borrowed much from other writers, and scholars have succeeded in tracing many of his sources. Such investigations can tell us much of Jonson's reading and of his habits of mind, but they cannot explain the power of the play. What is important is not what he borrowed, but what he made of his borrowings, and indeed the effect of *Volpone* is one of true originality. There is nothing really like *Volpone* elsewhere in English Literature, not even among Jonson's other writings. He succeeded in creating a particular world, with its own inhabitants. They relate, of course, to our own lives; all of us know what greed is, even if we are not ourselves, perhaps, greedy for wealth. *Volpone* can tell us something about the human heart, can make us understand how men may behave if they place material values above all others. Yet it makes us laugh at such men, even if there is some fear mixed with our laughter. And to make us fear, while at the same time we scorn, such evil obsessions is the true function of satirical comedy.

BEN JONSON

Volpone; Or, The Fox

NEVER, most equal Sisters, had any man a wit so presently excellent, as that it could raise itself; but there must come both matter, occasion, commenders, and favourers to it. If this be true, and that the fortune of all writers doth daily prove it, it behoves the careful to provide well toward these accidents; and, having acquired them, to preserve that part of reputation most tenderly, wherein the benefit of a friend is also defended. Hence is it, that I now render myself grateful, and am studious to justify the bounty of your act; to which, though your mere authority were satisfying, yet, it being an age wherein poetry 10 and the professors of it hear so ill on all sides, there will a reason be looked for in the subject. It is certain, nor can it with any forehead be opposed, that the too much license of poetasters in this time hath much deformed their mistress; that, every day, their manifold and manifest ignorance doth stick unnatural reproaches upon her: but for their petulancy, it were an act of the greatest injustice, either to let the learned suffer, or so divine a skill (which indeed should not be attempted with unclean

---

1 *presently:* immediately.   5 *accidents:* conditions.   11 *hear so ill:* are so badly spoken of.   13 *forehead:* boldness.   16 *petulancy:* impudence.

hands) to fall under the least contempt. For, if men will impar-
tially, and not asquint, look toward the offices and function of a
poet, they will easily conclude to themselves the impossibility
of any man's being the good poet, without first being a good
man. He that is said to be able to inform young men to all good
disciplines, inflame grown men to all great virtues, keep old men
in their best and supreme state, or, as they decline to childhood,
recover them to their first strength; that comes forth the inter-
preter and arbiter of nature, a teacher of things divine no less
than human, a master in manners; and can alone, or with a few,
effect the business of mankind: this, I take him, is no subject
for pride and ignorance to exercise their railing rhetoric upon.
But it will here be hastily answered, that the writers of these
days are other things; that not only their manners, but their
natures, are inverted, and nothing remaining with them of the
dignity of poet, but the abused name, which every scribe
usurps; that now, especially in dramatic, or, as they term it,
stage-poetry, nothing but ribaldry, profanation, blasphemy, all
license of offence to God and man is practised. I dare not deny a
great part of this, and am sorry I dare not, because in some
men's abortive features (and would they had never boasted the
light) it is over true: but that all are embarked in this bold
adventure for hell, is a most uncharitable thought, and, uttered,
a more malicious slander. For my particular, I can, and from a
most clear conscience, affirm, that I have ever trembled to think
toward the least profaneness; have loathed the use of such foul
and unwashed bawdry, as is now made the food of the scene:
and, howsoever I cannot escape, from some, the imputation of
sharpness, but that they will say, I have taken a pride, or lust,
to be bitter, and not my youngest infant but hath come into the
world with all his teeth; I would ask of these supercilious
politics, what nation, society, or general order or state, I have
provoked? what public person? whether I have not in all these
preserved their dignity, as mine own person, safe? My works are

24 *disciplines:* studies.   27 *arbiter:* judge.   33 *inverted:* perverted.
39 *features:* creations.   42 *For my particular:* as far as I am concerned.
45 *scene:* stage.   51 *politics:* politicians, know-alls.

read, allowed, (I speak of those that are entirely mine,) look
into them. What broad reproofs have I used? where have I
been particular? where personal? except to a mimic, cheater,
bawd, or buffoon, creatures, for their insolencies, worthy to be
taxed? Yet to which of these so pointingly, as he might not
either ingenuously have confess'd, or wisely dissembled his disease? But it is not rumour can make men guilty, much less 60
entitle me to other men's crimes. I know that nothing can be
so innocently writ or carried, but may be made obnoxious to
construction; marry, whilst I bear mine innocence about me, I
fear it not. Application is now grown a trade with many; and
there are that profess to have a key for the deciphering of everything: but let wise and noble persons take heed how they be too
credulous, or give leave to these invading interpreters to be
over-familiar with their fames, who cunningly, and often,
utter their own virulent malice, under other men's simplest
meanings. As for those that will (by faults which charity hath 70
raked up, or common honesty concealed) make themselves a
name with the multitude, or (to draw their rude and beastly
claps) care not whose living faces they intrench with their petulant styles, may they do it without rival, for me! I choose rather
to live graved in obscurity, than share with them in so preposterous a fame. Nor can I blame the wishes of those severe and
wiser patriots, who providing the hurts these licentious spirits
may do in a state, desire rather to see fools and devils, and those
antique relics of barbarism retrieved, with all other ridiculous
and exploded follies, than behold the wounds of private men, of 80
princes and nations: for, as Horace makes Trebatius speak
among these,

— *Sibi quisque timet, quanquam est intactus, et odit.*

And men may justly impute such rages, if continued, to the
writer, as his sports. The increase of which lust in liberty,

---

54 *allowed:* licensed, approved. 55 *broad:* general. 58 *pointingly:* particularly. 62 *obnoxious to construction:* liable to misinterpretation.
64 *Application:* attribution of personal satire.   82 *Sibi . . . odit:*
everyone fears for himself, and is angry, even though he is uninjured.

together with the present trade of the stage, in all their misc'-line interludes, what learned or liberal soul doth not already abhor? where nothing but the filth of the time is uttered, and that with such impropriety of phrase, such plenty of solecisms, such dearth of sense, so bold prolepses, so racked metaphors, 9 with brothelry, able to violate the ear of a pagan, and blasphemy, to turn the blood of a Christian to water.

I cannot but be serious in a cause of this nature, wherein my fame and the reputations of divers honest and learned are the question; when a name so full of authority, antiquity, and all great mark, is (through their insolence) become the lowest scorn of the age; and those men subject to the petulancy of every vernaculous orator, that were wont to be the care of kings and happiest monarchs. This it is that hath not only rapt me to present indignation, but made me studious heretofore, and by 10 all my actions, to stand off from them; which may most appear in this my latest work, which you, most learned Arbitresses, have seen, judged, and, to my crown, approved; wherein I have laboured for their instruction and amendment, to reduce not only the ancient forms, but manners of the scene, the easiness, the propriety, the innocence, and last, the doctrine, which is the principal end of poesie, to inform men in the best reason of living. And though my catastrophe may, in the strict rigour of comic law, meet with censure, as turning back to my promise; I desire the learned and charitable critic, to have so much faith 11 in me, to think it was done of industry: for with what ease I could have varied it nearer his scale (but that I fear to boast my own faculty) I could here insert. But my special aim being to put the snaffle in their mouths, that cry out, We never punish vice in our interludes, &c. I took the more liberty: though not without some lines of example, drawn even in the ancients themselves, the goings out of whose comedies are not always joyful, but oft times the bawds, the servants, the rivals, yea, and the masters are mulcted; and fitly, it being the office of a comic poet

86 *misc'line:* mixed. 90 *prolepses:* anachronisms. 98 *vernaculous:* popular, scurrilous. 103 *to my crown:* to my honour. 119 *mulcted:* punished.

to imitate justice, and instruct to life, as well as purity of langu- 120
age, or stir up gentle affections: to which I shall take the occasion elsewhere to speak.

For the present, most reverenced Sisters, as I have cared to
be thankful for your affections past, and here made the understanding acquainted with some ground of your favours; let me
not despair their continuance, to the maturing of some worthier
fruits: wherein, if my muses be true to me, I shall raise the de-
spised head of poetry again, and stripping her out of those
rotten and base rags wherewith the times have adulterated her
form, restore her to her primitive habit, feature, and majesty, 130
and render her worthy to be embraced and kiss'd of all the
great and master-spirits of our world. As for the vile and sloth-
ful, who never affected an act worthy of celebration, or are so
inward with their own vicious natures, as they worthily fear
her, and think it a high point of policy to keep her in contempt,
with their declamatory and windy invectives; she shall out of
just rage incite her servants (who are *genus irritabile*) to spout
ink in their faces, that shall eat farther than their marrow into
their fames; and not Cinnamus the barber, with his art, shall
be able to take out the brands; but they shall live, and be read, 140
till the wretches die, as things worst deserving of themselves in
chief, and then of all mankind.

From my House in the Black-Friars,
    this 11th day of February, 1607

    139 *Cinnamus:* a barber referred to in Martial's Epigrams.

THE PERSONS OF THE PLAY

VOLPONE, *a Magnifico*
MOSCA, *his Parasite*
VOLTORE, *an Advocate*
CORBACCIO, *an old Gentleman*
CORVINO, *a Merchant*
SIR POLITIC WOULD-BE, *a Knight*
PEREGRINE, *a Gentleman traveller*
BONARIO, *a young Gentleman, son to* CORBACCIO

LADY WOULD-BE, *the Knight's wife*
CELIA, *the Merchant's wife*

NANO, *a Dwarf*
CASTRONE, *an Eunuch*
ANDROGYNO, *a Hermaphrodite*

AVOCATORI, *four Magistrates*
NOTARIO, *the Register*
COMMANDADORI, *Officers*
MERCATORI, *three Merchants*
SERVITORE, *a Servant*

MOB

WOMEN

*

THE SCENE
VENICE

Magnifico: a nobleman of Venice, a grandee
the Register: Registrar, secretary

6

Volpone
or
The Fox

THE ARGUMENT

V OLPONE, childless, rich, feigns sick, despairs,
O ffers his state to hopes of several heirs,
L ies languishing; his parasite receives
P resents of all, assures, deludes: then weaves
O ther cross plots, which ope themselves, are told.
N ew tricks for safety are sought; they thrive: when bold,
E ach tempts th' other again, and all are sold.

PROLOGUE

Now, luck yet send us, and a little wit
Will serve to make our play hit;
(According to the palates of the season)
Here is rhyme, not empty of reason:
This we were bid to credit, from our poet,
Whose true scope, if you would know it,
In all his poems, still hath been this measure,
To mix profit with your pleasure;
And not as some, whose throats, their envy failing,
Cry hoarsely, 'All he writes is railing':   10
And, when his plays come forth, think they can flout them
With saying he was a year about them.
To these there needs no lie, but this his creature,
Which was, two months since, no feature;
And, though he dares give them five lives to mend it,
'Tis known, five weeks fully penn'd it:

3 *the palates of the season:* the taste of the time. 5 *to credit:* to guarantee. 14 *no feature:* not in being.

From his own hand, without a coadjutor,
Novice, journeyman, or tutor.
Yet, thus much I can give you as a token
Of his play's worth: no eggs are broken,   20
Nor quaking custards with fierce teeth affrighted,
Wherewith your rout are so delighted;
Nor hales he in a gull, old ends reciting,
To stop gaps in his loose writing;
With such a deal of monstrous and forc'd action
As might make Bet'lem a faction:
Nor made he his play for jests stolen from each table,
But makes jests to fit his fable;
And so presents quick comedy refined,
As best critics have designed;   30
The laws of time, place, persons he observeth,
From no needful rule he swerveth.
All gall and copperas from his ink he draineth,
Only a little salt remaineth;
Wherewith he'll rub your cheeks till, red with laughter,
They shall look fresh a week after.

22 *your rout:* the mob.   23 *gull:* fool.   *old ends:* scraps of old plays.
28 *fable:* plot, story.   33 *copperas:* vitriol.   34 *salt:* wit.

ACT I

Scene I

[*A room in* VOLPONE'*s house*]
Enter VOLPONE *and* MOSCA

VOLP. Good morning to the day; and next, my gold.
  Open the shrine that I may see my saint.
    [MOSCA *draws aside the curtain, revealing piles of gold, plate,
    jewels, etc.*
  Hail the world's soul, and mine! More glad than is
  The teeming earth to see the long'd-for sun
  Peep through the horns of the celestial Ram,
  Am I, to view thy splendour darkening his:
  That lying here, amongst my other hoards,
  Show'st like a flame by night; or like the day
  Struck out of chaos when all darkness fled
  Unto the centre. O, thou son of Sol,   10
  But brighter than thy father, let me kiss,
  With adoration, thee, and every relic
  Of sacred treasure in this blessed room.
  Well did wise poets, by thy glorious name,
  Title that age which they would have the best;
  Thou being the best of things, and far transcending
  All style of joy in children, parents, friends,
  Or any other waking dream on earth.
  Thy looks when they to Venus did ascribe,
  They should have given her twenty thousand Cupids;   20
  Such are thy beauties and our loves! Dear saint,
  Riches, the dumb god, that giv'st all men tongues,
  That canst do nought, and yet mak'st men do all things;
  The price of souls; even hell, with thee to boot,

10 *Sol:* the Sun.   15 *that age:* the Golden Age.   17 *style:* kinds.
24 *to boot:* in addition.

9

Is made worth heaven! Thou art virtue, fame,
Honour, and all things else! Who can get thee,
He shall be noble, valiant, honest, wise —
MOS. And what he will, sir. Riches are in fortune
A greater good than wisdom is in nature.
VOLP. True, my beloved Mosca. Yet I glory   30
More in the cunning purchase of my wealth
Than in the glad possession, since I gain
No common way: I use no trade, no venture;
I wound no earth with ploughshares, fat no beasts
To feed the shambles; have no mills for iron,
Oil, corn, or men, to grind 'em into powder;
I blow no subtle glass, expose no ships
To threat'nings of the furrow-faced sea;
I turn no monies in the public bank,
Nor usure private —
MOS.   No, sir, nor devour   40
Soft prodigals. You shall ha' some will swallow
A melting heir as glibly as your Dutch
Will pills of butter, and ne'er purge for't;
Tear forth the fathers of poor families
Out of their beds, and coffin them alive
In some kind clasping prison, where their bones
May be forthcoming when the flesh is rotten.
But your sweet nature doth abhor these courses;
You loathe the widow's or the orphan's tears
Should wash your pavements, or their piteous cries   50
Ring in your roofs and beat the air for vengeance. —
VOLP. Right, Mosca, I do loathe it.
MOS.   And besides, sir,
You are not like the thresher that doth stand
With a huge flail, watching a heap of corn,
And, hungry, dares not taste the smallest grain,
But feeds on mallows, and such bitter herbs;

---

31 *purchase:* acquisition. 33 *venture:* speculation, commercial enter-
prise. 35 *shambles:* the slaughter-house. 41 *soft prodigals:* young,
foolish spendthrifts. 43 *ne'er purge for it:* need no digestive medicine.

Nor like the merchant who hath fill'd his vaults
With Romagnía, and rich Candian wines,
Yet drinks the lees of Lombard's vinegar:
You will not lie in straw whilst moths and worms   60
Feed on your sumptuous hangings and soft beds.
You know the use of riches, and dare give now,
From that bright heap to me, your poor observer,
Or to your dwarf, or your hermaphrodite,
Your eunuch, or what other household trifle
Your pleasure allows maint'nance. —

VOLP.   Hold thee, Mosca.
Take of my hand; thou strik'st on truth in all,
And they are envious term thee parasite.
Call forth my dwarf, my eunuch, and my fool,
And let 'em make me sport.   [*Exit* MOSCA
                    What should I do,   70
But cocker up my genius, and live free
To all delights my fortune calls me to?
I have no wife, no parent, child, ally
To give my substance to; but whom I make
Must be my heir: and this makes men observe me.
This draws new clients daily to my house,
Women and men of every sex and age,
That bring me presents, send me plate, coin, jewels,
With hope that when I die (which they expect
Each greedy minute) it shall then return   80
Tenfold upon them; whilst some, covetous
Above the rest, seek to engross me whole,
And counter-work the one unto the other,
Contend in gifts, as they would seem in love:
All which I suffer, playing with their hopes,
And am content to coin 'em into profit,

---

58 *Romagnia, Candian:* Rumney and Malmsey, sweet wines from
Greece and Crete (Candy).   59 *lees:* dregs.   *Lombard's vinegar:* sharp
wine from N. Italy.   66 *Hold thee:* stop there.   68 *term:* who
term.   71 *cocker up:* pamper.   75 *observe:* flatter, be obsequious to.
76 *clients:* suitors.   82 *engross:* monopolize.   83 *counter-work:* work
against each other, double-cross.   85 *suffer:* allow.

And look upon their kindness, and take more,
And look on that; still bearing them in hand,
Letting the cherry knock against their lips,
And draw it by their mouths, and back again.   90
How now!

Enter NANO, ANDROGYNO, CASTRONE, *and* MOSCA

NAN. Now, room for fresh gamesters who do will you to know,
  They do bring you neither play nor university show;
  And therefore do entreat you, that whatsoever they rehearse
  May not fare a whit the worse for the false pace of the verse.
  If you wonder at this, you will wonder more ere we pass,
  For know, here is enclos'd the soul of Pythagoras,
  That juggler divine, as hereafter shall follow:
  Which soul, fast and loose, sir, came first from Apollo,
  And was breath'd into Aethalides, Mercurius his son,
  Where it had the gift to remember all that ever was done. 100
  From thence it fled forth, and made quick transmigration
  To goldy-lock'd Euphorbus who was kill'd in good fashion,
  At the siege of old Troy, by the cuckold of Sparta.
  Hermotimus was next (I find it in my charta)
  To whom it did pass, where no sooner it was missing
  But with one Pyrrhus of Delos it learn'd to go a-fishing:
  And thence did it enter the sophist of Greece.
  From Pythagore she went into a beautiful piece
  Hight Aspasia the meretrix; and the next toss of her
  Was again of a whore, she became a philosopher,   110
  Crates the cynic, as itself doth relate it;
  Since, kings, knights, and beggars, knaves, lords and fools
      gat it,
  Besides ox and ass, camel, mule, goat, and brock,
  In all which it hath spoke, as in the cobbler's cock.
  But I come not here to discourse of that matter,
  Or his one, two, or three, or his great oath, 'By Quater!'
  His musics, his trigon, his golden thigh,

91 *gamesters:* players. 94 *pace:* scansion. 104 *charta:* paper.
113 *brock:* badger. 117 *trigon:* triangular musical instrument.

Or his telling how elements shift; but I
Would ask how of late thou hast suffered translation,
And shifted thy coat in these days of reformation?   120
AND. Like one of the reformed, a fool as you see,
  Counting all old doctrine heresy.
NAN. But not on thine own forbid meats hast thou ventur'd?
AND. On fish, when first a Carthusian I enter'd.
NAN. Why, then thy dogmatical silence hath left thee?
AND. Of that an obstreperous lawyer bereft me.
NAN. O wonderful change! when sir lawyer forsook thee,
  For Pythagore's sake, what body then took thee?
AND. A good dull mule.
NAN.   And how! by that means
  Thou wert brought to allow of the eating of beans?   130
AND. Yes.
NAN.   But, from the mule, into whom did'st thou pass?
AND. Into a very strange beast, by some writers called an ass;
  By others, a precise, pure, illuminate brother
  Of those devour flesh, and sometimes one another:
  And will drop you forth a libel, or a sanctified lie,
  Betwixt every spoonful of a nativity-pie.
NAN. Now quit thee, 'fore heaven, of that profane nation,
  And gently report thy next transmigration.
AND. To the same that I am.
NAN.   A creature of delight?
  And (what is more than a fool) an hermaphrodite?   140
  Now 'pray thee, sweet soul, in all thy variation,
  Which body would'st thou choose to take up thy station?
AND. Troth this I am in, even here would I tarry.
NAN. 'Cause here the delight of each sex thou canst vary?
AND. Alas, those pleasures be stale and forsaken;
  No, 'tis your Fool, wherewith I am so taken,
  The only one creature that I can call blessed:

119 *translation:* change.   121 *one of the reformed:* a Protestant.
122 *old doctrine:* the teaching of the Church before the Reformation.
133 *a precise pure illuminate brother:* a Puritan.   136 *nativity-pie:*
Christmas pie (the Puritans objected to the word 'Christmas').

For all other forms I have proved most distressed.
NAN. Spoke true, as thou wert in Pythagoras still.
    This learned opinion we celebrate will,   150
    Fellow eunuch, as behoves us, with all our wit and art,
    To dignify that whereof ourselves are so great and special a
      part.

VOLP. Now very, very pretty: Mosca, this
    Was thy invention?
MOS.   If it please my patron,
    Not else.
VOLP. It doth, good Mosca.
MOS.   Then it was, sir.

NANO and CASTRONE sing

    Fools, they are the only nation
    Worth men's envy or admiration;
    Free from care or sorrow-taking,
    Selves and others merry making:
    All they speak or do is sterling.   160
    Your fool, he is your great man's darling
    And your ladies' sport and pleasure;
    Tongue and bauble are his treasure.
    E'en his face begetteth laughter,
    And he speaks truth free from slaughter;
    He's the grace of every feast,
    And sometimes the chiefest guest:
    Hath his trencher and his stool,
    When wit waits upon the fool.
      O, who would not be   170
        He, he, he?
                     [*Knocking without*

VOLP. Who's that? away, look, Mosca.
                [*Exeunt* NANO *and* CASTRONE
        Fool, begone. [*Exit* ANDROGYNO

165 *free from slaughter:* without being punished. **168** *trencher:* dish.

MOS. 'Tis Signior Voltore the advocate,
  I know him by his knock.
VOLP.   Fetch me my gown,
  My furs and night-caps; say my couch is changing,
  And let him entertain himself awhile
  Without, i' th' gallery.   [*Exit* MOSCA
                  Now, now, my clients
  Begin their visitation! Vulture, kite,
  Raven, and gorcrow, all my birds of prey,
  That think me turning carcase, now they come: 180
  I am not for 'em yet.

       Re-enter MOSCA *with the gown, etc.*

          How now? the news?
MOS. A piece of plate, sir.
VOLP.   Of what bigness?
MOS.   Huge,
  Massy and antique, with your name inscrib'd,
  And arms engraven.
VOLP.   Good! and not a fox
  Stretch'd on the earth, with fine delusive sleights,
  Mocking a gaping crow? ha, Mosca?
MOS.   Sharp, sir.
VOLP. Give me my furs. Why dost thou laugh so, man?
MOS. I cannot choose, sir, when I apprehend
  What thoughts he has without now, as he walks:
  That this might be the last gift he should give;   190
  That this would fetch you; if you died to-day,
  And gave him all, what he should be to-morrow;
  What large return would come of all his ventures;
  How he should worshipp'd be, and reverenc'd;
  Ride with his furs and foot-cloths, waited on
  By herds of fools and clients; have clear way
  Made for his mule, as letter'd as himself;

175 *my couch is changing:* my bed is being made. 179 *gorcrow:* carrion crow. 185 *delusive sleights:* deceiving tricks. 191 *fetch you:* catch you, win you over. 197 *letter'd:* learned.

Be call'd the great and learned advocate:
And then concludes there's nought impossible.
VOLP. Yes, to be learned, Mosca.
MOS.   O, no! rich   200
Implies it. Hood an ass with reverend purple,
So you can hide his two ambitious ears,
And he shall pass for a cathedral doctor.
VOLP. My caps, my caps, good Mosca, fetch him in.
MOS. Stay, sir, your ointment for your eyes.
VOLP.   That's true
Dispatch, dispatch: I long to have possession
Of my new present.
MOS.   That, and thousands more,
I hope to see you lord of.
VOLP.   Thanks, kind Mosca.
MOS. And that, when I am lost in blended dust,
And hundreds such as I am, in succession —   210
VOLP. Nay, that were too much, Mosca.
MOS.   You shall live
Still to delude these harpies.
VOLP.   Loving Mosca!
'Tis well, my pillow now, and let him enter.   [*Exit* MOSCA
Now, my feigned cough, my phthisick and my gout,
My apoplexy, palsy, and catarrhs,
Help, with your forced functions, this my posture,
Wherein, this three year, I have milk'd their hopes.
He comes, I hear him — Uh, uh, uh, uh! — Oh!

Re-enter MOSCA *with* VOLTORE

MOS. You still are what you were, sir. Only you,
Of all the rest, are he commands his love   220
And you do wisely to preserve it thus,
With early visitation and kind notes
Of your good meaning to him, which, I know,

202 *ambitious:* proud, 'stuck-up' like a donkey's ears.   203 *cathedral
doctor:* a Doctor of Divinity.   214 *phthisick:* cough, consumption.
216 *posture:* pose.

Cannot but come most grateful. Patron, sir!
Here's Signior Voltore is come —
VOLP.   What say you?
MOS. Sir, Signior Voltore is come, this morning,
    To visit you.
VOLP.   I thank him.
MOS.   And hath brought
    A piece of antique plate, bought of St. Mark,
    With which he here presents you.
VOLP.   He is welcome.
    Pray him to come more often.
MOS.   Yes.
VOLT.   What says he?   230
MOS. He thanks you, and desires you see him often.
VOLP. Mosca.
MOS.   My patron?
VOLP.   Bring him near, where is he?
    I long to feel his hand.
MOS.   The plate is here, sir.
VOLT. How fare you, sir?
VOLP.   I thank you, Signior Voltore.
    Where is the plate? mine eyes are bad.
VOLT.   I'm sorry
    To see you still thus weak.
MOS. [aside]   That he is not weaker.
VOLP. You are too munificent.
VOLT.   No, sir, would to heaven
    I could as well give health to you, as that plate.
VOLP. You give, sir, what you can. I thank you. Your love
    Hath taste in this, and shall not be unanswer'd.   240
    I pray you see me often.
VOLT.   Yes, I shall, sir.
VOLP. Be not far from me.
MOS.   Do you observe that, sir?
VOLP. Harken unto me, still: It will concern you.

228 *of St. Mark:* bought in St. Mark's Square in Venice.   240 *hath taste in this:* shows itself in this.

C

MOS. You are a happy man, sir; know your good.
VOLP. I cannot now last long —
MOS. [*aside*]   You are his heir, sir.
VOLT. [*aside*] Am I?
VOLP.   I feel me going — uh, uh, uh, uh!

[*Coughing*

    I am sailing to my port, — uh, uh, uh, uh! —
    And I am glad I am so near my haven.
MOS. Alas, kind gentleman; well, we must all go —
VOLT. But, Mosca —
MOS.   Age will conquer.   250
VOLT. 'Pray thee hear me.
    Am I inscrib'd his heir, for certain?
MOS.   Are you?
    I do beseech you, sir, you will vouchsafe
    To write me i' your family. All my hopes
    Depend upon your worship. I am lost
    Except the rising sun do shine on me.
VOLT. It shall both shine and warm thee, Mosca.
MOS.   Sir,
    I am a man that have not done your love
    All the worst offices: here I wear your keys,
    See all your coffers and your caskets lock'd,   260
    Keep the poor inventory of your jewels,
    Your plate, and monies, am your steward, sir,
    Husband your goods here.
VOLT.   But am I sole heir?
MOS. Without a partner, sir, confirm'd this morning;
    The wax is warm yet, and the ink scarce dry
    Upon the parchment.
VOLT.   Happy, happy me!
    By what good chance, sweet Mosca?
MOS.   Your desert, sir;
    I know no second cause.
VOLT.   Thy modesty

253–4 *vouchsafe to write me i' your family:* be good enough to take me into your household. 259 *offices:* services. 267 *desert:* merit.

Is loth to know it; well, we shall requite it.

MOS. He ever lik'd your course, sir; that first took him.   270
  I oft have heard him say how he admir'd
  Men of your large profession, that could speak
  To every cause, and things mere contraries,
  Till they were hoarse again, yet all be law;
  That with most quick agility could turn,
  And return; make knots, and undo them; .
  Give forked counsel; take provoking gold
  On either hand, and put it up: these men,
  He knew, would thrive with their humility.
  And, for his part, he thought he should be blest   280
  To have his heir of such a suffering spirit,
  So wise, so grave, of so perplex'd a tongue,
  And loud withal, that would not wag, nor scarce
  Lie still, without a fee; when every word
  Your worship but lets fall is a *cecchine*!

                              [*Knocking without*
  Who's that? one knocks; I would not have you seen, sir,
  And yet — pretend you came and went in haste;
  I'll fashion an excuse. And, gentle sir,
  When you do come to swim in golden lard,
  Up to the arms in honey, that your chin   290
  Is borne up stiff with fatness of the flood,
  Think on your vassal; but remember me:
  I ha' not been your worst of clients.

VOLT.   Mosca —

MOS. When will you have your inventory brought, sir?
  Or see a copy of the will? — Anon! —
  I'll bring 'em to you, sir. Away, begone,
  Put business i' your face.   [*Exit* VOLTORE

VOLP.   Excellent, Mosca!
  Come hither, let me kiss thee.

272 *large:* noble.   276 *knots:* difficulties.   277 *forked counsel:* am-
biguous advice. *provoking gold:* bribes.   278 *put it up:* pocket it.
282 *perplex'd:* complicated, involved.   283 *withal:* as well.   285 *cecchine:*
a Venetian gold coin.   297 *put business in your face:* look as if you have
been here on business.

MOS.   Keep you still, sir.
　Here is Corbaccio.
VOLP.   Set the plate away,
　The vulture's gone, and the old raven's come.   300
MOS. Betake you to your silence and your sleep:
　Stand there, and multiply. Now shall we see
　A wretch who is indeed more impotent
　Than this can feign to be; yet hopes to hop
　Over his grave.

Enter CORBACCIO

　　　　Signior Corbaccio!
　You're very welcome, sir.
CORB.   How does your patron?
MOS. Troth, as he did, sir, no amends.
CORB.   What? mends he?
MOS. No, sir: he is rather worse.
CORB.   That's well.
　Where is he?
MOS.   Upon his couch, sir, newly fall'n asleep.
CORB. Does he sleep well?
MOS.   No wink, sir, all this night,   310
　Nor yesterday, but slumbers.
CORB.   Good! He should take
　Some counsel of physicians: I have brought him
　An opiate here, from mine own doctor —
MOS. He will not hear of drugs.
CORB.   Why? I myself
　Stood by while 'twas made, saw all th' ingredients;
　And know it cannot but most gently work.
　My life for his, 'tis but to make him sleep.
VOLP. [*aside*] Aye, his last sleep, if he would take it.
MOS.   Sir,

302 *multiply*: increase (Mosca is putting down the gold plate which
Voltore brought). 304 *this*: Volpone. 307 *no amends*: no improve-
ment. 311 *but slumbers*: only naps.

He has no faith in physic.

CORB.   Say you? say you?

MOS. He has no faith in physic: he does think   320
　　Most of your doctors are the greater danger,
　　And worse disease, t' escape. I often have
　　Heard him protest that your physician
　　Should never be his heir.

CORB.   Not I his heir?

MOS. Not your physician, sir.

CORB.   O, no, no, no,
　　I do not mean it.

MOS.   No, sir, nor their fees
　　He cannot brook: he says they flay a man
　　Before they kill him.

CORB.   Right, I do conceive you.

MOS. And then they do it by experiment;
　　For which the law not only doth absolve 'em,   330
　　But gives them great reward; and he is loth
　　To hire his death so.

CORB.   It is true, they kill
　　With as much licence as a judge.

MOS.   Nay, more;
　　For he but kills, sir, where the law condemns,
　　And these can kill him too.

CORB.   Aye, or me,
　　Or any man. How does his apoplex?
　　Is that strong on him still?

MOS.   Most violent.
　　His speech is broken, and his eyes are set,
　　His face drawn longer than 'twas wont —

CORB.   How? how?
　　Stronger than he was wont?

MOS.   No, sir: his face   340
　　Drawn longer than 'twas wont.

CORB.   O, good.

MOS.   His mouth

338 *set:* fixed.

Is ever gaping, and his eyelids hang.
CORB.   Good.
MOS. A freezing numbness stiffens all his joints,
  And makes the colour of his flesh like lead.
CORB.   'Tis good.
MOS. His pulse beats slow and dull.
CORB.   Good symptoms still.
MOS. And from his brain —
CORB.   Ha? how? not from his brain?
MOS. Yes, sir, and from his brain —
CORB.   I conceive you, good.
MOS. Flows a cold sweat, with a continual rheum,
  Forth the resolved corners of his eyes.
CORB. Is 't possible? yet I am better, ha!   350
  How does he with the swimming of his head?
MOS. O, sir, 'tis past the scotomy; he now
  Hath lost his feeling, and hath left to snort:
  You hardly can perceive him that he breathes.
CORB. Excellent, excellent, sure I shall outlast him:
  This makes me young again, a score of years.
MOS. I was a-coming for you, sir.
CORB.   Has he made his will?
  What has he given me?
MOS.   No, sir.
CORB.   Nothing? ha?
MOS. He has not made his will, sir.
CORB.   Oh, oh, oh.
  What then did Voltore, the lawyer, here?   360
MOS. He smelt a carcass, sir, when he but heard
  My master was about his testament;
  (As I did urge him to it, for your good) —
CORB. He came unto him, did he? I thought so.
MOS. Yes, and presented him this piece of plate.
CORB. To be his heir?
MOS.   I do not know, sir.

348 *rheum:* catarrh.   349 *resolved:* weeping.   352 *scotomy:* dizziness.
353 *left:* ceased.

CORB.   True,
  I know it too.
MOS. [*aside*]   By your own scale, sir.
CORB.   Well,
  I shall prevent him yet. See, Mosca, look,
  Here I have brought a bag of bright *cecchines*
  Will quite weigh down his plate.
MOS.   Yea, marry, sir!   370
  This is true physic, this your sacred medicine,
  No talk of opiates to this great elixir.
CORB. 'Tis *aurum palpabile*, if not *potabile*.
MOS. It shall be minister'd to him in his bowl.
CORB. Aye, do, do, do.
MOS.   Most blessed cordial!
  This will recover him.
CORB.   Yes, do, do, do.
MOS. I think it were not best, sir.
CORB.   What?
MOS.   To recover him.
CORB. O, no, no, no; by no means.
MOS.   Why, sir, this
  Will work some strange effect, if he but feel it.
CORB. 'Tis true, therefore forbear. I'll take my venture: 380
  Give me 't again.
MOS.   At no hand, pardon me;
  You shall not do yourself that wrong, sir. I
  Will so advise you, you shall have it all.
CORB. How?
MOS.   All, sir, 'tis your right, your own; no man
  Can claim a part: 'tis yours, without a rival,
  Decreed by destiny.
CORB.   How, how, good Mosca?
MOS. I'll tell you, sir. This fit he shall recover —
CORB. I do conceive you.

367 *By your own scale*: from your knowledge of your own intentions.
368 *prevent*: forestall.   370 *weight down*: outweigh.   380 *venture*:
chance.   381 *at no hand*: by no means.

MOS.   And, on first advantage
  Of his gain'd sense, will I re-importune him
  Unto the making of his testament: 390
  And show him this.

CORB.   Good, good.

MOS.   'Tis better yet,
  If you will hear, sir.

CORB.   Yes, with all my heart.

MOS. Now would I counsel you, make home with speed;
  There, frame a Will: whereto you shall inscribe
  My master your sole heir.

CORB.   And disinherit
  My son?

MOS. O, sir, the better: for that colour
  Shall make it much more taking.

CORB.   O, but colour?

MOS. This Will, sir, you shall send it unto me.
  Now, when I come to enforce, as I will do,
  Your cares, your watchings, and your many prayers,   400
  Your more than many gifts, your this day's present,
  And last, produce your Will; where, without
    thought,
  Or least regard unto your proper issue,
  A son so brave and highly meriting,
  The stream of your diverted love hath thrown you
  Upon my master, and made him your heir:
  He cannot be so stupid, or stone dead,
  But, out of conscience and mere gratitude —

CORB. He must pronounce me his?

MOS.   'Tis true.

CORB.   This plot
  Did I think on before.

MOS.   I do believe it.   410

388-9 *on first advantage of his gain'd sense:* as soon as he has regained
his senses. 389 *re-importune:* entreat him again. 396 *colour:* pretence
(Corbaccio says 'O, but colour' = 'only a pretence'). 399 *enforce:*
emphasize. 403 *proper issue:* own child. 408 *mere:* simple.

CORB. Do you not believe it?

MOS.   Yes, sir.

CORB.   Mine own project.

MOS. Which when he hath done, sir —

CORB.   Publish'd me his heir?

MOS. And you so certain to survive him —

CORB.   Aye.

MOS. Being so lusty a man —

CORB.   'Tis true.

MOS.   Yes, sir —

CORB. I thought on that too. See how he should be
    The very organ to express my thoughts!

MOS. You have not only done yourself a good —

CORB. But multiplied it on my son?

MOS.   'Tis right, sir.

CORB. Still my invention.

MOS.   'Las, sir, heaven knows,
    It hath been all my study, all my care.   430 *(420 in margin)*
    (I e'en grow grey withal), how to work things —

CORB. I do conceive, sweet Mosca.

MOS.   You are he
    For whom I labour here.

CORB.   Aye, do, do, do:
    I'll straight about it.

MOS. [aside]   Rook go with you, raven!

CORB. I know thee honest.

MOS.   You do lie, sir —

CORB.   And —

MOS. Your knowledge is no better than your ears, sir.

CORB. I do not doubt to be a father to thee.

MOS. Nor I to gull my brother of his blessing.

CORB. I may ha' my youth restor'd to me, why not?

MOS. Your worship is a precious ass —

CORB.   What say'st thou?   430

MOS. I do desire your worship to make haste, sir.

---

424 *rook go with you:* may you be rooked, or cheated.   428 *gull:* cheat
out of.

CORB. 'Tis done, 'tis done, I go. [*Exit*

VOLP. [*leaping from his couch*]   O, I shall burst!
Let out my sides, let out my sides —

MOS.   Contain
Your flux of laughter, sir: you know this hope
Is such a bait it covers any hook.

VOLP. O, but thy working, and thy placing it!
I cannot hold; good rascal, let me kiss thee:
I never knew thee in so rare a humour.

MOS. Alas, sir, I but do as I am taught;
Follow your grave instructions, give 'em words,   440
Pour oil into their ears, and send them hence.

VOLP. 'Tis true, 'tis true. What a rare punishment
Is avarice to itself!

MOS.   Aye, with our help, sir.

VOLP. So many cares, so many maladies,
So many fears attending on old age,
Yea, death so often call'd on, as no wish
Can be more frequent with 'em, their limbs faint,
Their senses dull, their seeing, hearing, going,
All dead before them; yea, their very teeth,
Their instruments of eating, failing them: 450
Yet this is reckon'd life! Nay, here was one,
Is now gone home, that wishes to live longer!
Feels not his gout nor palsy, feigns himself
Younger by scores of years, flatters his age
With confident belying it, hopes he may,
With charms, like Aeson, have his youth restor'd:
And with these thoughts so battens as if fate
Would be so easily cheated on as he,
And all turns air! [*Another knocks*] Who's that, there, now? a
third?

MOS. Close, to your couch again: I hear his voice.   460
It is Corvino, our spruce merchant.

VOLP. [*lying down as before*]   Dead.

434 *flux:* fit. 441 *pour oil into their ears:* flatter them. 454 *flatters:*
conceals. 457 *battens:* stuffs himself.

MOS. Another bout, sir, with your eyes. [*Anoints them*] Who's
   there?

Enter CORVINO

   Signior Corvino! come most wish'd for! O,
   How happy were you, if you knew it, now!
CORV. Why? what? wherein?
MOS.   The tardy hour is come, sir.
CORV. He is not dead?
MOS.   Not dead, sir, but as good;
   He knows no man.
CORV.   How shall I do, then?
MOS.   Why, sir?
CORV. I have brought him here a pearl.
MOS.   Perhaps he has
   So much remembrance left as to know you, sir;
   He still calls on you, nothing but your name   470
   Is in his mouth. Is your pearl orient, sir?
CORV. Venice was never owner of the like.
VOLP. Signior Corvino!
MOS.   Hark.
VOLP.   Signior Corvino!
MOS. He calls you; step and give it him. He's here, sir,
   And he has brought you a rich pearl.
CORV.   How do you, sir?
   Tell him it doubles the twelve carat.
MOS.   Sir,
   He cannot understand, his hearing's gone;
   And yet it comforts him to see you —
CORV.   Say
   I have a diamond for him, too.
MOS.   Best show 't, sir,
   Put it into his hand; 'tis only there   480
   He apprehends: he has his feeling yet.
   See how he grasps it!

462 *another bout:* another go at. 465 *the tardy hour has come:* the
moment has come at last. 471 *orient:* of the finest quality.

CORV.   'Las, good gentleman!
   How pitiful the sight is!
MOS.   Tut, forget, sir.
   The weeping of an heir should still be laughter
   Under a visor.
CORV.   Why? am I his heir?
MOS. Sir, I am sworn I may not show the will,
   Till he be dead. But here has been Corbaccio,
   Here has been Voltore, here were others too,
   I cannot number 'em, they were so many,
   All gaping here for legacies; but I,   490
   Taking the vantage of his naming you,
   'Signior Corvino, Signior Corvino', took
   Paper and pen, and ink, and there I ask'd him
   Whom he would have his heir? 'Corvino'. Who
   Should be executor? 'Corvino'. And
   To any question he was silent to,
   I still interpreted the nods he made
   (Through weakness) for consent: and sent home th' others,
   Nothing bequeath'd them, but to cry and curse.
CORV. O, my dear Mosca! [*They embrace*] Does he not perceive
   us?   500
MOS. No more than a blind harper. He knows no man,
   No face of friend, nor name of any servant,
   Who 't was that fed him last, or gave him drink:
   Not those he hath begotten or brought up
   Can he remember.
CORV.   Has he children?
MOS.   Bastards,
   Some dozen or more, that he begot on beggars,
   Gipsies, and Jews, and black-moors, when he was drunk.
   Knew you not that, sir? 'Tis the common fable,
   The dwarf, the fool, the eunuch, are all his;
   H' is the true father of his family,   510
   In all save me: but he has given 'em nothing.
CORV. That's well, that's well. Art sure he does not hear us?

485 *visor:* mask. 491 *vantage:* advantage. 508 *fable:* story, rumour.

MOS. Sure, sir? why, look you, credit your own sense.
   [*to* VOLPONE] The pox approach, and add to your diseases,
   If it would send you hence the sooner, sir.
   For your incontinence it hath deserv'd it
   Throughly and throughly, and the plague to boot.
   (You may come near, sir) — Would you would once close
   Those filthy eyes of yours, that flow with slime,
   Like two frog-pits; and those same hanging cheeks,   520
   Cover'd with hide instead of skin — (Nay, help, sir) —
   That look like frozen dish-clouts set on end!
CORV. Or like an old smok'd wall, on which the rain
   Ran down in streaks.
MOS.   Excellent, sir, speak out;
   You may be louder yet: a culverin
   Discharged in his ear would hardly bore it.
CORV. His nose is like a common sewer, still running.
MOS. 'Tis good! and what his mouth?
CORV.   A very draught.
MOS. O, stop it up —
CORV.   By no means.
MOS.   'Pray you, let me.
   Faith, I could stifle him rarely with a pillow,   530
   As well as any woman that should keep him.
CORV. Do as you will, but I'll be gone.
MOS.   Be so;
   It is your presence makes him last so long.
CORV. I pray you, use no violence.
MOS.   No, sir? why?
   Why should you be thus scrupulous, 'pray you, sir?
CORV. Nay, at your discretion.
MOS.   Well, good sir, begone.
CORV. I will not trouble him now, to take my pearl?
MOS. Puh, nor your diamond. What a needless care
   Is this afflicts you? Is not all here yours?
   Am not I here, whom you have made your creature?   540

---

522 *dish-clouts*: dishcloths.   525 *culverin*: a large cannon.   526 *bore it*:
pierce it.   528 *draught*: a cess-pool.   531 *keep*: nurse.

That owe my being to you?

CORV.   Grateful Mosca!
Thou art my friend, my fellow, my companion,
My partner, and shalt share in all my fortunes.

MOS. Excepting one.

CORV.   What's that?

MOS.   Your gallant wife, sir.   [*Exit* CORVINO
Now is he gone: we had no other means
To shoot him hence but this.

VOLP.   My divine Mosca!
Thou hast to-day outgone thyself. [*Another knocks*] Who's
    there?
I will be troubled with no more. Prepare
Me music, dances, banquets, all delights;
The Turk is not more sensual in his pleasures   550
Than will Volpone.   [*Exit* MOSCA
                Let me see, a pearl?
A diamond? plate? chequins? Good morning's purchase
Why, this is better than rob churches, yet;
Or fat, by eating, once a month, a man —

Re-enter MOSCA

Who is 't?

MOS.   The most beauteous Lady Would-be, sir,
Wife to the English knight, Sir Politic Would-be,
(This is the style, sir, is directed me)
Hath sent to know how you have slept tonight
And if you would be visited.

VOLP.   Not now.
Some three hours hence —

MOS.   I told the squire so much.   560

VOLP. When I am high with mirth and wine: then, then.
'Fore heaven, I wonder at the desperate valour

552 *purchase:* booty, gain.   557 *style:* name and title.   560 *squire:*
manservant (the term is often used in Elizabethan English for a bawd
or pimp).

Of the bold English that they dare let loose
Their wives to all encounters!
MOS.   Sir, this knight
    Had not his name for nothing, he is politic,
    And knows, howe'er his wife affect strange airs,
    She hath not yet the face to be dishonest.
    But, had she Signior Corvino's wife's face —
VOLP. Has she so rare a face?
MOS.   O, sir, the wonder,
    The blazing star of Italy! a wench   570
    O' the first year! a beauty ripe as harvest!
    Whose skin is whiter than a swan, all over!
    Than silver, snow, or lilies! a soft lip
    Would tempt you to eternity of kissing!
    And flesh that melteth in the touch to blood!
    Bright as your gold! and lovely as your gold!
VOLP. Why had not I known this before?
MOS.   Alas, sir,
    Myself but yesterday discover'd it.
VOLP. How might I see her?
MOS.   O, not possible;
    She's kept as warily as is your gold;   580
    Never does come abroad, never takes air
    But at a window. All her looks are sweet
    As the first grapes or cherries, and are watch'd
    As near as they are.
VOLP.   I must see her —
MOS.   Sir,
    There is a guard of ten spies thick upon her,
    All his whole household: each of which is set
    Upon his fellow, and have all their charge,
    When he goes out, when he comes in, examin'd.
VOLP. I will go see her, though but at her window.

571 *O' the first year:* of the finest vintage.   584 *near:* closely.
586 *set:* put to spy.   587–8 *have all their charge ... examin'd:* each
of the servants is made to watch another, and questioned about his
movements.

MOS. In some disguise, then.

VOLP.   That is true. I must   590
  Maintain mine own shape still the same: we'll think.

[*Exeunt*

ACT II

Scene I

[St. Mark's Place: a retired corner before CORVINO's *house]*
Enter POLITIC WOULD-BE *and* PEREGRINE

POL. Sir, to a wise man, all the world's his soil.
  It is not Italy nor France nor Europe
  That must bound me, if my fates call me forth.
  Yet, I protest, it is no salt desire
  Of seeing countries, shifting a religion,
  Nor any disaffection to the state
  Where I was bred, and unto which I owe
  My dearest plots, hath brought me out; much less
  That idle, antique, stale, grey-headed project
  Of knowing men's minds and manners, with Ulysses: 10
  But a peculiar humour of my wife's
  Laid for this height of Venice, to observe,
  To quote, to learn the language, and so forth —
  I hope you travel, sir, with licence?
PER.   Yes.
POL. I dare the safelier converse — How long, sir,
  Since you left England?
PER.   Seven weeks.
POL.   So lately!
  You ha' not been with my lord ambassador?
PER. Not yet, sir.
POL.   'Pray you, what news, sir, vents our climate?
  I heard last night a most strange thing reported
  By some of my lord's followers, and I long   20
  To hear how 'twill be seconded!
PER.   What was 't, sir?

4 *salt:* extravagant.   5 *shifting:* changing.   18 *vents our climate:* is
published in our country.   21 *seconded:* confirmed.

D   33

POL. Marry, sir, of a raven, that should build
  In a ship royal of the king's.
PER. [*aside*]   This fellow
  Does he gull me, trow? or is gull'd? Your name, sir?
POL. My name is Politic Would-be.
PER. [*aside*]   O, that speaks him.
  A knight, sir?
POL.   A poor knight, sir.
PER.   Your lady
  Lies here in Venice for intelligence
  Of tires, and fashions, and behaviour,
  Among the courtezans? the fine Lady Would-be?
POL. Yes, sir, the spider and the bee oft-times   30
  Suck from one flower.
PER.   Good Sir Politic!
  I cry you mercy; I have heard much of you:
  'Tis true, sir, of your raven.
POL.   On your knowledge?
PER. Yes, and your lions whelping in the Tower.
POL. Another whelp!
PER.   Another, sir.
POL.   Now, heaven!
  What prodigies be these? The fires at Berwick!
  And the new star! these things concurring, strange,
  And full of omen! Saw you those meteors?
PER. I did, sir.
POL.   Fearful! 'Pray you, sir, confirm me,
  Were there three porpoises seen above the bridge,   40
  As they give out?
PER.   Six, and a sturgeon, sir.
POL. I am astonish'd!
PER.   Nay, sir, be not so;
  I'll tell you a greater prodigy than these —
POL. What should these things portend!

24 *trow:* do you think?   25 *that speaks him:* that describes him.
27 *lies:* stays. *intelligence:* news. 28 *tires:* head-dresses. 38 *full of
omen:* ominous. 44 *portend:* mean, prophesy.

PER.   The very day
  (Let me be sure) that I put forth from London
  There was a whale discover'd, in the river,
  As high as Woolwich, that had waited there,
  Few know how many months, for the subversion
  Of the Stode fleet.
POL.   Is 't possible? Believe it,
  'Twas either sent from Spain, or the Archduke's!   50
  Spinola's whale, upon my life, my credit!
  Will they not leave these projects? Worthy sir,
  Some other news.
PER.   Faith, Stone, the fool, is dead;
  And they do lack a tavern fool, extremely.
POL. Is Mass' Stone dead!
PER.   He's dead, sir; why, I hope
  You thought him not immortal? [*Aside*] O, this knight,
  Were he well known, would be a precious thing
  To fit our English stage: he that should write
  But such a fellow, should be thought to feign
  Extremely, if not maliciously.
POL.   Stone dead!   60
PER. Dead. Lord! how deeply, sir, you apprehend it!
  He was no kinsman to you?
POL.   That I know of.
  Well! that same fellow was an unknown fool.
PER. And yet you knew him, it seems?
POL.   I did so, sir,
  I knew him one of the most dangerous heads
  Living within the state, and so I held him.
PER. Indeed, sir?
POL.   While he liv'd, in action.
  He has receiv'd weekly intelligence,
  Upon my knowledge, out of the Low Countries,
  For all parts of the world, in cabbages;   70
  And those dispens'd again to ambassadors,

48 *subversion:* overthrow. 52 *projects:* inventions. 55 *Mass':* Master.
58 *fit:* suit.

In oranges, musk-melons, apricots,
Lemons, pome-citrons, and such-like: sometimes
In Colchester oysters, and your Selsey cockles.
PER. You make me wonder!
POL.   Sir, upon my knowledge.
Nay, I have observ'd him at your public ordinary
Take his advertisement from a traveller,
A conceal'd statesman, in a trencher of meat:
And, instantly, before the meal was done,
Convey an answer in a toothpick.
PER.   Strange!   80
How could this be, sir?
POL.   Why, the meat was cut
So like his character, and so laid, as he
Must easily read the cypher.
PER.   I have heard
He could not read, sir.
POL.   So 'twas given out,
In policy, by those that did employ him:
But he could read, and had your languages,
And to 't as sound a noddle —
PER.   I have heard, sir,
That your baboons were spies; and that they were
A kind of subtle nation near to China.
POL. Aye, aye, your Mamuluchi. Faith, they had   90
Their hand in a French plot or two; but they
Were so extremely given to women as
They made discovery of all: yet I
Had my advices here, on Wednesday last,
From one of their own coat, they were return'd,
Made their relations as the fashion is,
And now stand fair for fresh employment.
PER. [aside]   'Heart!
This Sir Pol will be ignorant of nothing. —

72 *musk-melons:* true melons (as distinct from water-melons). 73 *pome-citrons:* citron-apples.   76 *ordinary:* tavern.   77 *advertisement:* information. 82 *character:* cipher. *as:* that. 94 *advices:* dispatches. 95 *of their own coat:* one of their number. 96 *relations:* reports.

It seems, sir, you know all?

POL.   Not all, sir. But
I have some general notions; I do love   100
To note and to observe: though I live out,
Free from the active torrent, yet I'd mark
The currents and the passages of things
For mine own private use; and know the ebbs
And flows of state.

PER.   Believe it, sir, I hold
Myself in no small tie unto my fortunes
For casting me thus luckily upon you;
Whose knowledge, if your bounty equal it,
May do me great assistance, in instruction
For my behaviour, and my bearing, which   110
Is yet so rude and raw —

POL.   Why, came you forth
Empty of rules for travel?

PER.   Faith, I had
Some common ones, from out that vulgar grammar
Which he that cried Italian to me taught me.

POL. Why, this it is that spoils all our brave bloods,
Trusting our hopeful gentry unto pedants,
Fellows of outside, and mere bark. You seem
To be a gentleman of ingenuous race —
I not profess it, but my fate hath been
To be where I have been consulted with,   120
In this high kind, touching some great men's sons,
Persons of blood and honour —

Enter MOSCA *and* NANO *disguised, followed by persons with
materials for erecting a stage*

PER.   Who be these, sir?

MOS. Under that window, there 't must be. The same.

POL. Fellows to mount a bank! Did your instructor
In the dear tongues never discourse to you

---

106 *tie:* obligation.   114 *cried:* pronounced.   118 *ingenuous race:* good
birth.   125 *dear tongues:* choice languages.

Of the Italian mountebanks?

PER.   Yes, sir.

POL.   Why,
    Here shall you see one.

PER.   They are quacksalvers,
    Fellows that live by venting oils and drugs?

POL. Was that the character he gave you of them?

PER. As I remember.

POL.   Pity his ignorance.   130
    They are the only knowing men of Europe!
    Great general scholars, excellent physicians,
    Most admir'd statesmen, profess'd favourites,
    And cabinet counsellors to the greatest princes!
    The only languag'd men of all the world!

PER. And I have heard they are most lewd impostors;
    Made all of terms and shreds; no less beliers
    Of great men's favours than their own vile med'cines,
    Which they will utter upon monstrous oaths,
    Selling that drug for twopence, ere they part,   140
    Which they have valu'd at twelve crowns before.

POL. Sir, calumnies are answer'd best with silence.
    Yourself shall judge, Who is it mounts, my friends?

MOS. Scoto of Mantua, sir.

POL.   Is't he? Nay, then
    I'll proudly promise, sir, you shall behold
    Another man than has been phant'sied to you.
    I wonder, yet, that he should mount his bank
    Here in this nook, that has been wont t' appear
    In face of the Piazza! Here he comes.

Enter VOLPONE, *disguised as a mountebank doctor, and followed*
                      by a mob of people

VOLP. [*to* NANO]   Mount, zany.

MOB. Follow, follow, follow, follow, follow.   150

----

128 *venting:* dispensing.   135 *languag'd men:* orators.   136 *lewd:*
ignorant.   137 *terms and shreds:* technical jargon and scraps of
knowledge. 137 *beliers:* false boasters. 139 *utter:* sell. 146 *phant'sied:*
represented.   148 *zany:* fool, stooge.

POL. See how the people follow him! He's a man
    May write ten thousand crowns in bank here.

                   [VOLPONE *mounts the stage*
                      Note,

    Mark but his gesture: I do use to observe
    The state he keeps in getting up!
PER.   'Tis worth it, sir.
VOLP. 'Most noble gentlemen and my worthy patrons, it may
    seem strange that I, your Scoto Mantuano who was ever wont
    to fix my bank in face of the public Piazza, near the shelter
    of the Portico to the Procuratia, should now, after eight
    months' absence from this illustrious city of Venice, humbly
    retire myself into an obscure nook of the Piazza.'   160
POL. Did not I now object the same?
PER.   Peace, sir.
VOLP. 'Let me tell you: I am not, as your Lombard proverb
    saith, cold on my feet; or content to part with my commodi-
    ties at a cheaper rate than I accustomed: look not for it.
    Nor that the calumnious reports of that impudent detractor
    and shame to our profession (Alessandro Buttone, I mean),
    who gave out in public I was condemn'd a sforzato to the
    galleys, for poisoning the Cardinal Bembo's cook, hath at all
    attached, much less dejected me. No, no, worthy gentlemen;
    to tell you true, I cannot endure to see the rabble of these 170
    ground *ciarlitani*, that spread their cloaks on the pavement
    as if they meant to do feats of activity and then come in
    lamely with their mouldy tales out of Boccaccio, like stale
    Tabarine, the fabulist: some of them discoursing their
    travels, and of their tedious captivity in the Turks' galleys,
    when indeed, were the truth known, they were the Christians'
    galleys, where very temperately they ate bread, and drank
    water, as a wholesome penance, enjoin'd them by their con-
    fessors, for base pilferies.'

154 *state:* dignity. 168 *sforzato:* prisoner sentenced to hard labour.
169 *attached:* had any effect on. 171 *ciarlitani:* charlatans, inferior
cheapjacks who performed on the ground, not on stages. 172 *feats
of activity:* gymnastics. 174 *fabulist:* story-teller.

POL. Note but his bearing, and contempt of these.   18

VOLP. 'These turdy-facy-nasty-paty-lousy-fartical rogues,
with one poor groat's-worth of unprepar'd antimony, finely
wrapt up in several *scartoccios*, are able, very well, to kill
their twenty a week, and play; yet these meagre starv'd
spirits, who have half stopp'd the organs of their minds with
earthy oppilations, want not their favourers among your
shrivell'd, salad-eating artisans, who are overjoy'd that they
may have their half-pe'rth of physic; though it purge 'em
into another world, 't makes no matter.'

POL. Excellent! ha' you heard better language, sir?   19

VOLP. 'Well, let 'em go. And gentlemen, honourable gentlemen, know that for this time, our bank, being thus remov'd
from the clamours of the *canaglia*, shall be the scene of
pleasure and delight: for I have nothing to sell, little or
nothing to sell.'

POL. I told you, sir, his end.

PER.   You did so, sir.

VOLP. 'I protest, I, and my six servants, are not able to make of
this precious liquor so fast as it is fetch'd away from my
lodging by gentlemen of your city; strangers of the *terra-
firma*; worshipful merchants; aye, and senators too: who 20
ever since my arrival have detained me to their uses by their
splendidous liberalities. And worthily. For what avails your
rich man to have his magazines stuff'd with *moscadelli*, or of
the purest grape, when his physicians prescribe him, on pain
of death, to drink nothing but water cocted with aniseeds?
O, health! health! the blessing of the rich! the riches of the
poor! who can buy thee at too dear a rate, since there is no
enjoying this world without thee? Be not then so sparing of
your purses, honourable gentlemen, as to abridge the natural
course of life —'   21

PER. You see his end?

183 *scartoccio:* piece of paper.   186 *oppilations:* obstructions.
188 *half-pe'rth:* halfpennyworth.   193 *canaglia:* rabble, mob, *canaille.*
199 *terra-firma:* the mainland (Venice is built on islands). 203 *moscaselli:*
muscadel, sweet wine.   205 *cocted:* boiled.

POL.　　　　　　　Aye, is't not good?

VOLP. 'For when a humid flux, or catarrh, by the mutability of
air, falls from your head into an arm or shoulder, or any
other part, take you a ducat, or your *cecchine* of gold, and
apply to the place affected: see what good effect it can work.
No, no, 'tis this blessed *unguento*, this rare extraction, that
hath only power to disperse all malignant humours that
proceed either of hot, cold, moist, or windy causes —'

PER. I would he had put in dry too.

POL.　　　　　　　　　　　　'Pray you, observe.

VOLP. 'To fortify the most indigest and crude stomach, aye, 220
were it of one that through extreme weakness vomited blood,
applying only a warm napkin to the place, after the unction
and fricace; for the *vertigine* in the head, putting but a drop
into your nostrils, likewise behind the ears; a most sovereign
and approved remedy: the *malcaducco*, cramps, convulsions,
paralyses, epilepsies, *tremor-cordia*, retired nerves, ill
vapours of the spleen, stoppings of the liver, the stone, the
strangury, *hernia ventosa, iliaca passio*; stops a dysenteria
immediately; easeth the torsion of the small guts; and cures
melancholia hypocondriaca, being taken and applied accord- 230
ing to my printed receipt. [*Pointing to his bill and his glass*]
For this is the physician, this the medicine; this counsels,
this cures; this gives the direction, this works the effect; and,
in sum, both together may be term'd an abstract of the theo-
ric and practic in the Aesculapian art. 'Twill cost you eight
crowns. And, Zan Fritada, 'pray thee sing a verse extempore
in honour of it.'

---

216 *unguento:* ointment.　220 *indigest and crude:* dyspeptic, of weak
digestion.　222 *unction:* application of ointment.　223 *fricace:* rubbing,
massage.　223 *vertigine:* giddiness.　225 *malcaducco:* 'falling sickness',
epilepsy.　226 *tremor-cordia:* palpitations of the heart.　*retired nerves:*
shrunken sinews.　227 *ill vapours of the spleen:* melancholia arising
from disease of the spleen (supposed to be the seat of melancholy).
228 *hernia ventosa:* rupture.　*iliaca passio:* colic.　229 *torsion of
the small guts:* pains in the stomach.　230 *melancholia hypochondriaca:*
'windy melancholy', supposed to arise from disorder of the organs
below the ribs.　231 *receipt:* prescription.　235 *Aesculapian art:* the
art of healing.

POL. How do you like him, sir?

PER.   Most strangely, I!

POL. Is not his language rare?

PER.   But alchemy,

   I never heard the like: or Broughton's books.   24

NANO sings

     Had old Hippocrates, or Galen,
     That to their books put med'cines all in,
     But known this secret, they had never
     (Of which they will be guilty ever)
     Been murderers of so much paper,
     Or wasted many a hurtless taper:
     No Indian drug had e'er been famed,
     Tobacco, sassafras not named;
     Ne yet of guacum one small stick, sir,
     Nor Raymund Lully's great elixir.   25
     Ne had been known the Danish Gonswart,
     Or Paracelsus, with his long sword.

PER. All this, yet, will not do; eight crowns is high.

VOLP. 'No more — Gentlemen, if I had but time to discourse to you the miraculous effects of this my oil, surnamed Oglio del Scoto; with the countless catalogue of those I have cured of th' aforesaid and many more diseases; the patents and privileges of all the princes and commonwealths of Christendom; or but the depositions of those that appear'd on my part before the signiory of the Sanità and most learned 26 College of Physicians; where I was authorized, upon notice taken of the admirable virtues of my medicaments, and mine own excellency in matter of rare and unknown secrets, not only to disperse them publicly in this famous city but in all the territories that happily joy under the government of the

239 But alchemy: except in alchemical works.   248 sassafras: a kind of medicinal bark.   249 guacum: drug made from the resin of a West Indian tree.   251 Ne: nor.   259 depositions: testimonials. 260 the signiory of the Sanità: the Public Health committee of Venice. 264 disperse: distribute.

most pious and magnificent states of Italy. But may some
other gallant fellow say, O, there be divers that make profession to have as good and as experimented receipts as yours.
Indeed, very many have essay'd, like apes in imitation of that
which is really and essentially in me, to make of this oil, be- 270
stow'd great cost in furnaces, stills, alembecks, continual
fires, and preparation of the ingredients (as indeed there goes
to it six hundred several simples, besides some quantity of
human fat, for the conglutination, which we buy of the ana-
tomists), but, when these practitioners come to the last decoction, blow, blow, puff, puff, and all flies *in fumo*: ha, ha,
ha! Poor wretches! I rather pity their folly and indiscretion
than their loss of time and money: for those may be recovered by industry: but to be a fool born is a disease
incurable. For myself, I always from my youth have 280
endeavoured to get the rarest secrets, and book them, either
in exchange or for money: I spared nor cost nor labour
where anything was worthy to be learned. And gentlemen,
honourable gentlemen, I will undertake, by virtue of chemical
art, out of the honourable hat that covers your head, to
extract the four elements; that is to say, the fire, air, water,
and earth, and return you your felt without burn or stain.
For, whil'st others have been at the balloo, I have been at my
book: and am now past the craggy paths of study and come to
the flowery plains of honour and reputation.'   290
POL. I do assure you, sir, that is his aim.
VOLP. 'But to our price.'
PER.   And that withal, Sir Pol.
VOLP. 'You all know, honourable gentlemen, I never valued
this *ampulla*, or vial, at less than eight crowns, but for this
time I am content to be depriv'd of it for six; six crowns is
the price, and less in courtesy I know you cannot offer me:
take it or leave it, howsoever, both it and I am at your service.
I ask you not as the value of the thing, for then I should

271 *alembecks:* alembics, distilling apparatus.   273 *simples:* medicinal
herbs.   275 *decoction:* boiling down.   276 *in fumo:* in smoke.
288 *balloo:* a Venetian ball-game.

demand of you a thousand crowns, so the Cardinals Montalto, Fernese, the great Duke of Tuscany, my gossip, with 300 divers other princes have given me; but I despise money. Only to show my affection to you, honourable gentlemen, and your illustrious state here, I have neglected the messages of these princes, mine own offices, fram'd my journey hither, only to present you with the fruits of my travels. Tune your voices once more to the touch of your instruments, and give the honourable assembly some delightful recreation.'

PER. What monstrous, and most painful circumstance
    Is here, to get some three or four gazettes!
    Some three pence, i' th' whole, for that 'twill come to.   310

NANO *sings*

You that would last long, list to my song,
Make no more coil, but buy of this oil.
Would you be ever fair and young?
Stout of teeth and strong of tongue?
Tart of palate, quick of ear?
Sharp of sight, of nostril clear?
Moist of hand and light of foot?
Or, I will come nearer to 't,
Would you live free from all diseases?
Do the act your mistress pleases,   320
Yet fright all aches from your bones?
Here's a med'cine for the nones.

VOLP. 'Well, I am in a humour at this time to make a present of the small quantity my coffer contains: to the rich in courtesy and to the poor for God's sake. Wherefore, now mark; I ask'd you six crowns; and six crowns, at other times, you have paid me; you shall not give me six crowns, nor five, nor four, nor three, nor two, nor one; nor half a ducat; no, nor a *moccinigo*: sixpence it will cost you, or six hundred pound —

---

300 *gossip:* friend.   309 *gazette:* a Venetian coin, worth about three farthings.   312 *coil:* fuss.   315 *tart of palate:* of sharp appetite. 322 *for the nones:* for the occasion. 329 *moccinigo:* a coin worth about 9d.

expect no lower price, for by the banner of my front, I will not 330
bate a *bagatine*; that I will have, only, a pledge of your loves,
to carry something from amongst you to show I am not
contemn'd by you. Therefore, now, toss your handkerchiefs,
cheerfully, cheerfully; and be advertised that the first heroic
spirit that deigns to grace me with a handkerchief, I will give
it a little remembrance of something beside, shall please it
better than if I had presented it with a double pistolet.'

PER. Will you be that heroic spark, Sir Pol?

　　　　　[CELIA *at the window throws down her handkerchief*
O, see! the window has prevented you.

VOLP. Lady, I kiss your bounty: and, for this timely grace you 340
have done your poor Scoto of Mantua, I will return you, over
and above my oil, a secret of that high and inestimable
nature shall make you for ever enamour'd on that minute
wherein your eye first descended on so mean (yet not altogether to be despis'd) an object. Here is a powder conceal'd
in this paper, of which, if I should speak to the worth, nine
thousand volumes were but as one page, that page as a line,
that line as a word: so short is this pilgrimage of man (which
some call life) to the expressing of it. Would I reflect on the
price? why, the whole world were but as an empire, that 350
empire as a province, that province as a bank, that bank as a
private purse to the purchase of it. I will only tell you it is the
powder that made Venus a goddess (given her by Apollo),
that kept her perpetually young, clear'd her wrinkles, firm'd
her gums, fill'd her skin, colour'd her hair; from her deriv'd
to Helen, and at the sack of Troy unfortunately lost: till now,
in this our age, it was as happily recover'd by a studious
antiquary out of some ruins of Asia, who sent a moiety of
it to the court of France (but much sophisticated) wherewith
the ladies there now colour their hair. The rest, at this 360
present, remains with me, extracted to a quintessence: so

330 *the banner of my front:* his flag, which he compares to the standard
of an army.　331 *bagatine:* coin worth about one third of a farthing.
337 *pistolet:* a Spanish gold coin, worth about 18s.　339 *prevented:*
forestalled.　358 *moiety:* half.　359 *sophisticated:* corrupt, mixed with
other things.

that, wherever it but touches, in youth it perpetually pre-
serves, in age restores the complexion; seats your teeth, did
they dance like virginal jacks, firm as a wall; makes them
white as ivory, that were black as —

Enter CORVINO

CORV. Spite o' the devil and my shame! come down, here;
  Come down: no house but mine to make your scene?
  Signior Flaminio, will you down, sir? down?
  What, is my wife your Franciscina, sir?
  No windows on the whole Piazza here   370
  To make your properties, but mine? but mine?
                            [*Beats away* VOLPONE, *etc.*
  Heart, ere tomorrow, I shall be new christen'd,
  And call'd the Pantalone di Besogniosi
  About the town.
PER.   What should this mean, Sir Pol?
POL. Some trick of state, believe it. I will home.
PER. It may be some design on you.
POL.   I know not.
  I'll stand upon my guard.
PER.   It is your best, sir.
POL. This three weeks, all my advices, all my letters,
  They have been intercepted.
PER.   Indeed, sir?
  Best have a care.
POL.   Nay, so I will.
PER.   This knight,   380
  I may not lose him, for my mirth, till night.   [*Exeunt*

364 *virginal jacks:* the pieces of wood which made the quills pluck the
strings of virginals, a kind of harpsichord (but Jonson may be thinking
of the keys, which would be white, like teeth).   375 *trick of state:* political device.

Scene II

[A room in VOLPONE's *house]*
Enter VOLPONE *and* MOSCA

VOLP. O, I am wounded.

MOS.   Where, sir?

VOLP.   Not without;
  Those blows were nothing: I could bear them ever.
  But angry Cupid, bolting from her eyes,
  Hath shot himself into me, like a flame,
  Where now he flings about his burning heat
  As in a furnace an ambitious fire
  Whose vent is stopp'd. The fight is all within me.
  I cannot live except thou help me, Mosca;
  My liver melts, and I, without the hope
  Of some soft air from her refreshing breath,   10
  Am but a heap of cinders.

MOS.   'Las, good sir!
  Would you had never seen her.

VOLP.   Nay, would thou
  Hadst never told me of her.

MOS.   Sir, 'tis true;
  I do confess, I was unfortunate,
  And you unhappy: but I am bound in conscience
  No less than duty to effect my best
  To your release of torment, and I will, sir.

VOLP. Dear Mosca, shall I hope?

MOS.   Sir, more than dear,
  I will not bid you to despair of aught
  Within a human compass.

VOLP.   O, there spoke   20
  My better angel. Mosca, take my keys,
  Gold, plate, and jewels, all's at thy devotion;
  Employ them how thou wilt; nay, coin me, too:
  So thou, in this, but crown my longings, Mosca!

---

3 *bolting:* shooting, like a bolt of arrow.   20 *compass:* scope, ability.

MOS. Use but your patience.

VOLP.   So I have.

MOS.   I doubt not
To bring success to your desires.

VOLP.   Nay, then,
I not repent me of my late disguise.

MOS. If you can horn him, sir, you need not.

VOLP.   True:
Besides, I never meant him for my heir.
Is not the colour o' my beard and eyebrows.   30
To make me known?

MOS.   No jot.

VOLP.   I did it well.

MOS. So well, would I could follow you in mine,
With half the happiness; [*aside*] and yet I would
Escape your epilogue.

VOLP.   But were they gull'd
With a belief that I was Scoto?

MOS.   Sir,
Scoto himself could hardly have distinguish'd!
I have not time to flatter you now, we'll part:
And as I prosper, so applaud my art.   [*Exeunt*

Scene III

[*A room in* CORVINO's *house*]
Enter CORVINO, *sword in hand, dragging in* CELIA

CORV. Death of mine honour, with the city's fool?
A juggling, tooth-drawing, prating mountebank?
And at a public window? where, whilst he,
With his strain'd action, and his dole of faces,
To his drug-lecture draws your itching ears,
A crew of old, unmarried, noted lechers,
Stood leering up like satyrs: and you smile

28 *horn him:* make a cuckold of him.   34 *epilogue:* i.e., the beating
which Corvino gave Volpone after his 'act'.   4 *action:* gestures. *dole
of faces:* change of expression, grimaces.

Most graciously and fan your favours forth,
To give your hot spectators satisfaction!
What, was your mountebank their call? their whistle?   10
Or were you enamour'd on his copper rings?
His saffron jewel, with the toad-stone in 't?
Or his embroider'd suit with the cope-stitch,
Made of a hearse-cloth? or his old tilt-feather?
Or his starch'd beard? Well! you shall have him, yes.
He shall come home, and minister unto you
The fricace for the mother. Or, let me see,
I think you'd rather mount; would you not mount?
Why, if you'll mount, you may; yes truly, you may:
And so you may be seen, down to the foot.   20
Get you a cittern, Lady Vanity,
And be a dealer with the virtuous man;
Make one: I'll but protest myself a cuckold,
And save your dowry. I am a Dutchman, I!
For, if you thought me an Italian,
You would be damn'd ere you did this, you whore!
Thou'dst tremble to imagine that the murder
Of father, mother, brother, all thy race,
Should follow, as the subject of my justice!
CEL. Good sir, have patience!
CORV.   What couldst thou propose   30
Less to thyself, than in this heat of wrath,
And stung with my dishonour, I should strike
This steel into thee with as many stabs
As thou wert gaz'd upon with goatish eyes?
CEL. Alas, sir! be appeas'd. I could not think
My being at the window should more now
Move your impatience than at other times.
CORV. No? not to seek and entertain a parley
With a known knave before a multitude?

12 *toad-stone:* semi-precious stone believed to be found in the head of a toad.   13 *cope-stitch:* stitch used in embroidering a clergyman's cope or cloak.   14 *tilt-feather:* feather from a knight's plume picked up after a tilt or joust.   17 *the mother:* hysteria.   21 *cittern:* stringed instrument, similar to a guitar.   38 *parley:* conference.

E

You were an actor with your handkerchief,   40
Which he most sweetly kissed in the receipt,
And might, no doubt, return it with a letter
And A'point the place where you might meet: your sister's,
Your mother's, or your aunt's might serve the turn.

CEL. Why, dear sir, when do I make these excuses,
  Or ever stir abroad, but to the church?
  And that so seldom —

CORV.   Well, it shall be less;
  And thy restraint before was liberty
  To what I now decree: and therefore mark me.
  First, I will have this bawdy light damm'd up;   50
  And till 't be done, some two or three yards off
  I'll chalk a line: o'er which if thou but chance
  To set thy desp'rate foot more hell, more horror,
  More wild remorseless rage shall seize on thee
  Than on a conjurer that had heedless left
  His circle's safety ere his devil was laid.
  Then here's a lock which I will hang upon thee;
  And, now I think on 't, I will keep thee backwards;
  Thy lodging shall be backwards; thy walks backwards;
  Thy prospect — all be backwards; and no pleasure   60
  That thou shalt know but backwards. Nay, since you force
  My honest nature, know it is your own
  Being too open makes me use you thus.
  Since you will not contain your subtle nostrils
  In a sweet room, but they must snuff the air
  Of rank and sweaty passengers — [Knock within]
                                    One knocks.
  Away, and be not seen, pain of thy life;
  Nor look toward the window: if thou dost —
  Nay, stay, hear this — let me not prosper, whore,
  But I will make thee an anatomy,   70

---

50 *light:* window. 55 *conjurer:* magician. 58 *keep thee backwards:*
i.e., in the rear part of the house. 66 *passengers:* passers-by. 70 *anatomy:* in the Renaissance public dissections of human bodies were often
given by Professors of Anatomy.

Dissect thee mine own self, and read a lecture
Upon thee, to the city and in public.
Away!   [*Exit* CELIA
      Who's there?

Enter SERVANT

SER.   'Tis Signior Mosca, sir.
CORV. Let him come in. [*Exit* SERVANT] His master's dead.
    There's yet
Some good to help the bad.

Enter MOSCA

              My Mosca, welcome!
I guess your news.
MOS.   I fear you cannot, sir.
CORV. Is't not his death?
MOS.   Rather the contrary.
CORV. Not his recovery?
MOS.   Yes, sir.
CORV.   I am curs'd,
    I am bewitch'd, my crosses meet to vex me.
    How? how? how? how?
MOS.   Why, sir, with Scoto's oil!   80
    Corbaccio and Voltore brought of it
    Whilst I was busy in an inner room —
CORV. Death! that damn'd mountebank! but for the law
    Now I could kill the rascal: 't cannot be
    His oil should have that virtue. Ha' not I
    Known him a common rogue, come fiddling in
    To th' *osteria*, with a tumbling whore,
    And, when he ha' done all his forc'd tricks, been glad
    Of a poor spoonful of dead wine, with flies in 't?
    It cannot be. All his ingredients   90
    Are a sheep's gall, a roasted bitch's marrow,
    Some few sod earwigs, pounded caterpillars,

79 *crosses:* disappointments. 87 *osteria:* inn. *tumbling whore:* female
acrobat. 92 *sod:* boiled.

A little capon's grease, and fasting spittle:
I know 'em, to a dram.

MOS.   I know not, sir,
But some on 't, there, they pour'd into his ears.
Some in his nostrils, and recover'd him,
Applying but the fricace.

CORV.   Pox o' that fricace!

MOS. And since, to seem the more officious
And flatt'ring of his health, there, they have had,
At extreme fees, the College of Physicians   100
Consulting on him, how they might restore him;
Where one would have a cataplasm of spices,
Another, a flay'd ape clapp'd to his breast,
A third would ha' it a dog, a fourth an oil,
With wild cats' skins: at last, they all resolv'd
That to preserve him was no other means
But some young woman must be straight sought out,
Lusty and full of juice, to sleep by him;
And to this service, most unhappily
And most unwillingly, am I now employ'd,   110
Which here I thought to pre-acquaint you with,
For your advice, since it concerns you most,
Because I would not do that thing might cross
Your ends, on whom I have my whole dependence, sir:
Yet, if I do it not, they may delate
My slackness to my patron, work me out
Of his opinion; and there all your hopes,
Ventures, or whatsoever, are all frustrate.
I do but tell you, sir. Besides, they are all
Now striving who shall first present him. Therefore —   120
I could entreat you, briefly conclude somewhat:
Prevent 'em if you can.

CORV.   Death to my hopes!
This is my villainous fortune! Best to hire
Some common courtesan.

93 *fasting spittle:* the spittle of someone who has been fasting.
98 *officious:* dutiful. 102 *cataplasm:* poultice. 115 *delate:* denounce.

MOS.   Aye, I thought on that, sir.
But they are all so subtle, full of art,
And age again doting and flexible,
So as — I cannot tell — we may perchance
Light on a quean may cheat us all.

CORV.   'Tis true.

MOS. No, no: it must be one that has no tricks, sir,
Some simple thing, a creature made unto it;   130
Some wench you may command. Ha' you no kinswoman?
Gods so — Think, think, think, think, think, think, think,
     sir.
One o' the doctors offer'd there his daughter.

CORV. How!

MOS.   Yes, Signior Lupo, the physician.

CORV. His daughter?

MOS.   And a virgin, sir. Why? Alas,
He knows the state of 's body what it is;
That nought can warm his blood, sir, but a fever,
Nor any incantation raise his spirit:
A long forgetfulness hath seiz'd that part.
Besides, sir, who shall know it? some one, or two —   140

CORV. I pray thee give me leave. [*Walks aside*] If any man
But I had this luck — The thing, in 'tself,
I know, is nothing — Wherefore should not I
As well command my blood and my affections
As this dull doctor? In the point of honour,
The cases are all one, of wife and daughter.

MOS. [*aside*] I hear him coming.

CORV. [*aside*]   She shall do 't: 'Tis done.
'Slight, if this doctor, who is not engag'd,
Unless't be for his counsel, which is nothing,
Offer his daughter, what should I, that am   150
So deeply in? I will prevent him. Wretch!
Covetous wretch! — Mosca, I have determin'd.

MOS. How, sir?

122 *prevent:* be before. 128 *quean:* wench. 148 *'Slight:* God's light.
151 *prevent:* forestall.

CORV.   We'll make all sure. The party you wot of
    Shall be mine own wife, Mosca.
MOS.   Sir, the thing,
    But that I would not seem to counsel you,
    I should have motion'd to you at the first:
    And, make your count, you have cut all their throats.
    Why! 'tis directly taking a possession!
    And, in his next fit, we may let him go.
    'Tis but to pull the pillow from his head,   160
    And he is throttled: 't had been done before
    But for your scrupulous doubts.
CORV.   Aye, a plague on 't,
    My conscience fools my wit. Well, I'll be brief,
    And so be thou, lest they should be before us;
    Go home, prepare him, tell him with what zeal
    And willingness I do it: swear it was
    On the first hearing, as thou mayst do truly,
    Mine own free motion.
MOS.   Sir, I warrant you,
    I'll so possess him with it that the rest
    Of his starv'd clients shall be banish'd all,   170
    And only you receiv'd. But come not, sir,
    Until I send, for I have something else
    To ripen for your good, you must not know't.
CORV. But do not you forget to send now.
MOS.   Fear not.   [Exit

                  Re-enter CELIA

CORV. Where are you, wife? my Celia wife! What, blubbering?
    Come dry those tears. I think thou thought'st me in earnest.
    Ha? By this light, I talked so but to try thee.
    Methinks the lightness of the occasion
    Should ha' confirm'd thee. Come, I am not jealous.
CEL. No?
CORV.   Faith, I am not, aye, nor never was: 180

156 *motion'd:* suggested. 157 *make your count:* be certain, count on
it. 178 *lightness:* frivolity. 179 *confirm'd:* reassured.

It is a poor unprofitable humour.
Do not I know, if women have a will,
They'll do 'gainst all the watches o' the world,
And that the fiercest spies are tamed with gold?
Tut, I am confident in thee; thou shalt see 't:
And see, I'll give thee cause, too, to believe it.
Come, kiss me. Go, and make thee ready straight,
In all thy best attire, thy choicest jewels,
Put 'em all on, and, with 'em, thy best looks:
We are invited to a solemn feast   190
At old Volpone's, where it shall appear
How far I am free from jealousy or fear.   [*Exeunt*

ACT III

Scene I

[*A street*]
Enter MOSCA

MOS. I fear I shall begin to grow in love
With my dear self, and my most prosp'rous parts,
They do so spring and burgeon; I can feel
A whimsy i' my blood: I know not how,
Success hath made me wanton. I could skip
Out of my skin now, like a subtle snake,
I am so limber. O! your parasite
Is a most precious thing, dropp'd from above,
Not bred 'mongst clods and clot-poles, here on earth.
I muse, the mystery was not made a science,   10
It is so liberally profess'd! almost
All the wise world is little else, in nature,
But parasites or sub-parasites. And yet
I mean not those that have your bare town-art,
To know who's fit to feed 'em; have no house,
No family, no care, and therefore mould
Tales for men's ears, to bait that sense; or get
Kitchen-invention and some stale receipts
To please the belly and the groin; nor those,
With their court dog-tricks, that can fawn and fleer,   20
Make their revenue out of legs and faces,
Echo my Lord, and lick away a moth:
But your fine elegant rascal, that can rise

3 *burgeon:* flourish, sprout.   4 *whimsy:* excitement.   5 *wanton:* gay.
7 *limber:* lithe, nimble.   10 *mystery:* profession.   17 *bait that sense:*
feed the love of gossip.   18 *receipts:* recipes.   21 *Make their revenue
. . . faces:* get their living by bowing and smirking.   22 *lick away a
moth:* i.e., from their Lord's clothes (moth may = mote; the words
were pronounced alike in Jacobean English).

And stoop, almost together, like an arrow;
Shoot through the air as nimbly as a star;
Turn short as doth a swallow; and be here,
And there, and here, and yonder, all at once;
Present to any humour, all occasion;
And change a visor swifter than a thought!
This is the creature had the art born with him;   30
Toils not to learn it, but doth practise it
Out of the most excellent nature: and such sparks
Are the true parasites, others but their zanies.

Enter BONARIO

Who's this? Bonario? old Corbaccio's son?
The person I was bound to seek. Fair Sir,
You are happ'ly met.
BON.   That cannot be by thee.
MOS. Why, sir?
BON.   Nay, 'pray thee know thy way, and leave me:
I would be loth to interchange discourse
With such a mate as thou art.
MOS.   Courteous sir,
Scorn not my poverty.
BON.   Not I, by heaven: 40
But thou shalt give me leave to hate thy baseness.
MOS. Baseness?
BON.   Aye, answer me, is not thy sloth
Sufficient argument? thy flattery?
Thy means of feeding?
MOS.   Heaven be good to me!
These imputations are too common, sir,
And eas'ly stuck on virtue, when she's poor;
You are unequal to me, and howe'er
Your sentence may be righteous, yet you are not,
That, ere you know me, thus proceed in censure:
St. Mark bear witness 'gainst you, 'tis inhuman. [*Weeps*] 50

28 *Present . . . occasion:* suit himself to any mood or event. 29 *visor:*
(feigned) expression. 39 *mate:* fellow, rogue. 47 *unequal:* unjust.

BON. [*aside*] What? does he weep? the sign is soft and good!
   I do repent me that I was so harsh.
MOS. 'Tis true that, sway'd by strong necessity,
   I am enforc'd to eat my careful bread
   With too much obsequy; 'tis true, beside,
   That I am fain to spin mine own poor raiment
   Out of my mere observance, being not born
   To a free fortune: but that I have done
   Base offices, in rending friends asunder,
   Dividing families, betraying counsels,   60
   Whispering false lies, or mining men with praises,
   Train'd their credulity with perjuries,
   Corrupted chastity, or am in love
   With mine own tender ease, but would not rather
   Prove the most rugged and laborious course
   That might redeem my present estimation;
   Let me here perish, in all hope of goodness.
BON. [*aside*] This cannot be a personated passion! —
   I was to blame, so to mistake thy nature;
   'Pray thee, forgive me and speak out thy business.   70
MOS. Sir, it concerns you; and though I may seem,
   At first, to make a main offence in manners,
   And in my gratitude unto my master,
   Yet for the pure love which I bear all right,
   And hatred of the wrong, I must reveal it.
   This very hour your father is in purpose
   To disinherit you —
BON.   How!
MOS.   And thrust you forth
   As a mere stranger to his blood; 'tis true, sir,
   The work no way engageth me, but as
   I claim an interest in the general state   80
   Of goodness and true virtue, which I hear

54 *careful:* got with difficulty and pain. 55 *obsequy:* obsequiousness.
57 *observance:* service, waiting on Volpone. 61 *mining:* under-mining,
ruining.   62 *train'd:* lured, deceived.   66 *estimation:* reputation.
68 *personated:* pretended.   72 *main:* grave, serious.

T' abound in you: and for which mere respect,
Without a second aim, sir, I have done it.

BON. This tale hath lost thee much of the late trust
   Thou hadst with me; it is impossible:
   I know not how to lend it any thought
   My father should be so unnatural.

MOS. It is a confidence that well becomes
   Your piety; and form'd, no doubt, it is
   From your own simple innocence: which makes   90
   Your wrong more monstrous and abhorr'd. But, sir,
   I now will tell you more. This very minute,
   It is, or will be doing: and, if you
   Shall be but pleas'd to go with me, I'll bring you,
   I dare not say where you shall see, but where
   Your ear shall be a witness of the deed;
   Hear yourself written bastard, and profess'd
   The common issue of the earth.

BON.   I'm 'maz'd!

MOS. Sir, if I do it not, draw your just sword,
   And score your vengeance on my front and face;   100
   Mark me your villain: You have too much wrong,
   And I do suffer for you, sir. My heart
   Weeps blood in anguish —

BON.   Lead. I follow thee.   *[Exeunt*

Scene II

[*A room in* VOLPONE'*s house*]
Enter VOLPONE

VOLP. Mosca stays long, methinks. Bring forth your sports
   And help to make the wretched time more sweet.

Enter NANO, ANDROGYNO, *and* CASTRONE

NAN. Dwarf, fool, and eunuch, well met here we be.

---

82 *for which mere respect:* with regard to which only. 98 *issue of the
earth:* fatherless, of unknown parentage. 100 *front:* forehead.
1 *sports:* entertainment.

A question it were now, whether of us three,
Being all the known delicates of a rich man,
In pleasing him, claim the precedency can?
CAS. I claim for myself.
AND.   And so doth the fool.
NAN. 'Tis foolish indeed: let me set you both to school.
First, for your dwarf, he's little and witty
And everything, as it is little, is pretty;   10
Else why do men say to a creature of my shape,
So soon as they see him, 'It's a pretty little ape'?
And, why a pretty ape but for pleasing imitation
Of greater men's actions, in a ridiculous fashion?
Beside, this feat body of mine doth not crave
Half the meat, drink, and cloth, one of your bulks will have.
Admit your fool's face be the mother of laughter,
Yet, for his brain, it must always come after:
And, though that do feed him, it's a pitiful case
His body is beholding to such a bad face.   [*One knocks*]   20
VOLP. Who's there? my couch; away, look, Nano see:
                    [*Exeunt* ANDROGYNO *and* CASTRONE
Give me my caps first — go, enquire.   [*Exit* NANO
                    Now, Cupid
Send it be Mosca, and with fair return.
NAN. [*within*] It is the beauteous Madam —
VOLP.   Would-be — is it?
NAN. The same.
VOLP.   Now torment on me! squire her in,
For she will enter or dwell here for ever.
Nay, quickly. [*retires to his couch*] That my fit were past! I
    fear
A second hell too, that my loathing this
Will quite expel my appetite to the other:
Would she were taking now her tedious leave.   30
Lord, how it threats me what I am to suffer!

Re-enter NANO *with* LADY POLITIC WOULD-BE

4 *whether:* which.   5 *delicates:* favourites.   15 *feat:* neat.

LADY P. I thank you, good sir. 'Pray you signify
  Unto your patron I am here. — This band
  Shows not my neck enough. — I trouble you, sir,
  Let me request you bid one of my women
  Come hither to me, [*Exit* NANO] In good faith, I am dress'd
  Most favourably to-day! It is no matter;
  'Tis well enough.

Re-enter NANO *with* WAITING-WOMAN

          Look, see these petulant things!
  How they have done this!
VOLP. [*aside*]   I do feel the fever
  Entering in at mine ears; O for a charm   40
  To fright it hence.
LADY P.   Come nearer: is this curl
  In his right place? or this? Why is this higher
  Than all the rest? you ha' not wash'd your eyes yet?
  Or do they not stand even i' your head?
  Where is your fellow? call her.   [*Exit* WOMAN
NAN.   Now St. Mark
  Deliver us! anon, she'll beat her women
  Because her nose is red.

Re-enter WAITING-WOMAN *with* SECOND WOMAN

LADY P.   I pray you, view
  This tire, forsooth: are all things apt or no?
WOM. One hair a little here sticks out, forsooth.
LADY P. Does't so, forsooth? and where was your dear sight 50
  When it did so, forsooth? What now? bird-ey'd?
  And you too? 'pray you both approach and mend it.
  Now, by that light, I muse you are not asham'd!
  I, that have preach'd these things so oft unto you,
  Read you the principles, argu'd all the grounds,
  Disputed every fitness, every grace,
  Call'd you to counsel of so frequent dressings —

33 *band:* collar. 38 *petulant:* impatient. 51 *bird-ey'd:* beady-eyed
(or perhaps ironical, since birds have sharp eyes).

NAN. [*aside*] More carefully than of your fame or honour.
LADY P. Made you acquainted what an ample dowry
  The knowledge of these things would be unto you,   60
  Able, alone, to get you noble husbands
  At your return: and you thus to neglect it!
  Besides, you seeing what a curious nation
  Th' Italians are, what will they say of me?
  'The English lady cannot dress herself.'
  Here's a fine imputation to our country!
  Well, go your ways, and stay i' the next room.
  This fucus was too coarse too; it's no matter. —
  Good sir, you'll give 'em entertainment?
                              [*Exeunt* NANO *and* WOMEN
VOLP. The storm comes toward me.
LADY P.   How does my Volpone?   70
VOLP. Troubled with noise, I cannot sleep; I dreamt
  That a strange fury entered now my house,
  And, with the dreadful tempest of her breath,
  Did cleave my roof asunder.
LADY P.   Believe me, and I
  Had the most fearful dream, could I remember 't —.
VOLP. [*aside*] Out on my fate! I ha' given her the occasion
  How to torment me: she will tell me hers.
LADY P. Methought the golden mediocrity,
  Polite and delicate —
VOLP.   O, if you do love me,
  No more; I sweat and suffer at the mention   80
  Of any dream: feel how I tremble yet.
LADY P. Alas, good soul! the passion of the heart.
  Seed-pearl were good now, boil'd with syrup of apples,
  Tincture of gold and coral, citron-pills,
  Your elicampane root, myrobalanes —
VOLP. [*aside*] Ah me, I have ta'en a grasshopper by the wing.

---

63 *curious:* fastidious.   68 *fucus:* rouge.   69 *give them entertainment:*
look after them.   82 *passion of the heart:* heartburn.   85 *elicampane:*
the herb 'horse-heal' (a species of Hellenium). *myrobalanes:* an oriental
fruit rather like a plum.

LADY P. Burnt silk and amber. You have muscadel
   Good i' the house —

VOLP.   You will not drink, and part?

LADY P. No, fear not that. I doubt we shall not get
   Some English saffron, half a dram would serve,   90
   Your sixteen cloves, a little musk, dried mints,
   Bugloss and barley-meal —

VOLP. [aside]   She's in again!
   Before I feign'd diseases, now I have one.

LADY P. And these appli'd with a right scarlet cloth

VOLP. [aside] Another flood of words! A very torrent!

LADY P. Shall I sir, make you a poultice?

VOLP.   No, no, no;
   I am very well: you need prescribe no more.

LADY P. I have a little studied physic; but now
   I am all for music: save, i' the forenoons,
   An hour or two for painting. I would have   100
   A lady, indeed, t' have all letters and arts,
   Be able to discourse, to write, to paint,
   But principal, as Plato holds, your music
   (And so does wise Pythagoras, I take it)
   Is your true rapture, when there is consent
   In face, in voice, and clothes: and is, indeed,
   Our sex's chiefest ornament.

VOLP.   The poet
   As old in time as Plato, and as knowing,
   Says that your highest female grace is silence.

LADY P. Which o' your poets? Petrarch? or Tasso? or
   Dante?   110
   Guarini? Ariosto? Aretine?
   Cieco di Hadria? I have read them all.

VOLP. [aside] Is everything a cause to my destruction?

LADY P. I think I ha' two or three of 'em about me.

VOLP. [aside] The sun, the sea will sooner both stand still
   Than her eternal tongue! Nothing can 'scape it.

LADY P. Here's *Pastor Fido* —

               105 *consent*: harmony.

VOLP. [*aside*]   Profess obstinate silence,
That's now my safest.
LADY P.   All our English writers,
I mean such as are happy in the Italian,
Will deign to steal out of this author, mainly;   120
Almost as much as from Montagnie:
He has so modern and facile a vein,
Fitting the time, and catching the court-ear.
Your Petrarch is more passionate, yet he,
In days of sonneting, trusted 'em with much:
Dante is hard, and few can understand him.
But for a desperate wit, there's Aretine!
Only his pictures are a little obscene —
You mark me not?
VOLP.   Alas, my mind's perturb'd.
LADY P. Why, in such cases, we must cure ourselves,   130
Make use of our philosophy —
VOLP.   Oh me.
LADY P. And, as we find our passions do rebel,
Encounter 'em with reason; or divert 'em
By giving scope unto some other humour
Of lesser danger: as, in politic bodies,
There's nothing more doth overwhelm the judgement,
And cloud the understanding, than too much
Settling and fixing and, as 't were, subsiding
Upon one object. For the incorporating
Of these same outward things into that part   140
Which we call mental leaves some certain faeces
That stop the organs, and, as Plato says,
Assassinates our knowledge.
VOLP. [*aside*]   Now the spirit
Of patience help me.
LADY P.   Come, in faith, I must
Visit you more a days and make you well:
Laugh and be lusty.

125 *trusted:* provided.   141 *faeces:* excrement, by-product.
145 *more a days:* more often.

VOLP. [*aside*]   My good angel save me!
LADY P. There was but one sole man in all the world
  With whom I e'er could sympathize; and he
  Would lie you often, three, four hours together
  To hear me speak: and be sometimes so rapt   150
  As he would answer me quite from the purpose,
  Like you, and you are like him, just. I'll discourse
  (And 't be but only, sir, to bring you asleep)
  How we did spend our time and loves together,
  For some six years.
VOLP.   Oh, oh, oh, oh, oh, oh!
LADY P. For we were *coaetanei*, and brought up —
VOLP. [*aside*] Some power, some fate, some fortune rescue me.

Enter MOSCA

MOS. God save you, Madam.
LADY P.   Good sir.
VOLP.   Mosca, welcome!
  [*Aside*] Welcome to my redemption.
MOS. [*aside*]   Why, sir?
VOLP. [*aside*]   Oh,
  Rid me of this my torture quickly there;   160
  My madam with the everlasting voice:
  The bells, in time of pestilence, ne'er made
  Like noise, or were in that perpetual motion;
  The cock-pit comes not near it. All my house,
  But now, steam'd like a bath with her thick breath.
  A lawyer could not have been heard; nor scarce
  Another woman, such a hail of words
  She has let it fall. For hell's sake, rid her hence.
MOS. Has she presented?
VOLP.   O, I do not care,
  I'll take her absence upon any price,   170
  With any loss.
MOS.   Madam —

---

  156 *coaetanei:* equals in age.   169 *presented:* made a present.
F

LADY P.   I ha' brought your patron
  A toy, a cap here, of mine own work —
MOS.   'Tis well.
  I had forgot to tell you, I saw your knight
  Where you'd little think it —
LADY P.   Where?
MOS.   Marry,
  Where yet, if you make haste, you may apprehend him,
  Rowing upon the water in a gondola
  With the most cunning courtesan of Venice.
LADY P. Is't true?
MOS.   Pursue 'em, and believe your eyes:
  Leave me to make your gift.
                          [*Exit* LADY POLITIC WOULD-BE *hastily*
                                    I knew 't would take.
  For lightly they that use themselves most licence   180
  Are still most jealous.
VOLP.   Mosca, hearty thanks
  For thy quick fiction and delivery of me.
  Now to my hopes, what say'st thou?

                  Re-enter LADY POLITIC WOULD-BE

LADY P.   But do you hear, sir? —
VOLP. [*aside*] Again! I fear a paroxysm.
LADY P.   Which way
  Row'd they together?
MOS.   Toward the Rialto.
LADY P. I pray you, lend me your dwarf.
MOS.   I pray you take him.   [*Exit* LADY P.
  Your hopes, sir, are like happy blossoms, fair,
  And promise timely fruit, if you will stay
  But the maturing; keep you at your couch,
  Corbaccio will arrive straight, with the will: 190
  When he is gone I'll tell you more.   [*Exit*
VOLP.   My blood,

          184 *paroxysm:* stroke.

My spirits are return'd; I am alive —
And like your wanton gamester at primero,
Whose thought had whisper'd to him not go less,
Methinks I lie and draw — for an encounter.

        [The curtains round VOLPONE's *bed are drawn*

      Enter MOSCA *and* BONARIO

MOS. Sir, here concealed, you may hear all. But 'pray you,
  Have patience, sir; [*Knocking within*] the same's your father
    knocks:
  I am compell'd to leave you.
BON.   Do so. Yet
  Cannot my thought imagine this a truth.

  BONARIO *is placed behind a curtain,* MOSCA *goes out and*
      re-enters with CORVINO *and* CELIA

MOS. Death on me! you are come too soon, what meant
    you?   200
  Did not I say I would send?
CORV.   Yes, but I feared
  You might forget it, and then they prevent us.
MOS. Prevent? [*aside*] Did e'er man haste so for his horns?
  A courtier would not ply it so for a place. —
  Well, now there is no helping it, stay here;
  I'll presently return.   [*Exit*
CORV.   Where are you, Celia?
  You know not wherefore I have brought you hither?
CEL. Not well, except you told me.
CORV.   Now I will:
  Hark hither.   [CORVINO *and* CELIA *go outside*

    MOSCA *comes back and speaks to* BONARIO

MOS.   Sir, your father hath sent word
  It will be half an hour ere he come;   210
  And therefore, if you please to walk the while
  Into that gallery — at the upper end,
  There are some books to entertain the time:

And I'll take care no man shall come unto you, sir.

BON. Yes, I will stay there. [*Aside, and exit*] I do doubt this
    fellow.

MOS. There, he is far enough; he can hear nothing:
    And, for his father, I can keep him off.   [*Exit*

CORVINO *comes forward dragging* CELIA

CORV. Nay, now, there is no starting back, and therefore
    Resolve upon it: I have so decreed.
    It must be done. Nor would I move 't afore,   220
    Because I would avoid all shifts and tricks
    That might deny me.

CEL.   Sir, let me beseech you,
    Affect not these strange trials; if you doubt
    My chastity, why, lock me up for ever;
    Make me the heir of darkness. Let me live
    Where I may please your fears, if not your trust.

CORV. Believe it, I have no such humour, I.
    All that I speak I mean; yet I am not mad:
    Not horn-mad, see you? Go to, show yourself
    Obedient, and a wife.

CEL.   O heaven!

CORV.   I say it,   230
    Do so.

CEL. Was this the train?

CORV.   I have told you reasons;
    What the physicians have set down; how much
    It may concern me; what my engagements are;
    My means; and the necessity of those means
    For my recovery: wherefore, if you be
    Loyal and mine, be won, respect my venture.

CEL. Before your honour?

CORV.   Honour? tut, a breath;
    There's no such thing in nature: a mere term
    Invented to awe fools. What, is my gold

229 *horn-mad:* mad with jealousy. 231 *train:* plot. 233 *engagements:*
debts.

The worse for touching? clothes, for being look'd on?   240
Why, this's no more. An old, decrepit wretch
That has no sense, no sinew; takes his meat
With others' fingers; only knows to gape
When you do scald his gums; a voice, a shadow;
And what can this man hurt you?
CEL. [*aside*]   Lord! what spirit
Is this hath entered him?
CORV.   And for your fame,
That's such a jig; as if I would go tell it,
Cry it on the Piazza! Who shall know it
But he that cannot speak it, and this fellow,
Whose lips are i' my pocket? Save yourself,   250
(If you'll proclaim 't, you may) I know no other
Should come to know it.
CEL.   Are heaven and saints then nothing?
Will they be blind or stupid?
CORV.   How?
CEL.   Good sir,
Be jealous still, emulate them; and think
What hate they burn with toward every sin.
CORV. I grant you: if I thought it were a sin
I would not urge you. Should I offer this
To some young Frenchman, or hot Tuscan blood
That had read Aretine, conn'd all his prints,
Knew every quirk within lust's labyrinth,   260
And were profess'd critic in lechery;
And I would look upon him and applaud him,
This were a sin: but here, 'tis contrary,
A pious work, mere charity for physic,
An honest polity to assure mine own.
CEL. O heaven! canst thou suffer such a change?
VOLP. [*aside*] Thou art mine honour, Mosca, and my pride,
My joy, my tickling, my delight! go, bring 'em.
MOS. [*comes forward*] Please you draw near, sir.
CORV.   Come on; what —

247 *jig:* farce.   260 *quirk:* twist.   265 *polity:* policy.

You will not be rebellious? By that light —   270
MOS. Sir, Signior Corvino here is come to see you.
VOLP. Oh!
MOS.   And hearing of the consultation had,
   So lately, for your health, is come to offer,
   Or rather, sir, to prostitute —
CORV.   Thanks, sweet Mosca.
MOS. Freely, unask'd, or unintreated —
CORV.   Well.
MOS. As the true fervent instance of his love
   His own most fair and proper wife; the beauty
   Only of price in Venice —
CORV.   'Tis well urg'd.
MOS. To be your comfortress, and to preserve you.
VOLP. Alas, I am past already! 'pray you, thank him   280
   For his good care and promptness, but for that,
   'Tis a vain labour, e'en to fight 'gainst heaven;
   Applying fire to a stone: [coughing] uh, uh, uh, uh! —
   Making a dead leaf grow again. I take
   His wishes gently, though; and you may tell him
   What I have done for him: marry, my state is hopeless!
   Will him to pray for me; and t' use his fortune
   With reverence, when he comes to 't.
MOS.   Do you hear, sir?
   Go to him with your wife.
CORV.   Heart of my father!
   Wilt thou persist thus? come, I pray thee, come.   290
   Thou seest 'tis nothing, Celia. By this hand,
   I shall grow violent. Come, do 't, I say.
CEL. Sir, kill me, rather: I will take down poison,
   Eat burning coals, do anything —
CORV.   Be damn'd.
   Heart, I will drag thee hence home by the hair;
   Cry thee a strumpet through the streets; rip up
   Thy mouth unto thine ears; and slit thy nose

278 *only of price:* most precious.   281 *but for that:* but as for that.

Like a raw rochet — Do not tempt me, come.
Yield, I am loth — Death! I will buy some slave
Whom I will kill, and bind thee to him alive;   300
And at my window hang you forth, devising
Some monstrous crime, which I, in capital letters,
Will eat into thy flesh with *aqua fortis*
And burning corsives, on this stubborn breast.
Now, by the blood thou hast incens'd, I'll do 't.

CEL. Sir, what you please, you may, I am your martyr.

CORV. Be not thus obstinate, I ha' not deserved it:
Think who it is entreats you. 'Pray thee, sweet;
Good faith, thou shalt have jewels, gowns, attires,
What thou wilt think and ask. Do but go kiss him,   310
Or touch him, but. For my sake. — At my suit
This once. No? not? I shall remember this.
Will you disgrace me thus? Do you thirst my undoing?

MOS. Nay, gentle lady, be advis'd.

CORV.   No, no.
She has watch'd her time. God's precious, this is scurvy;
'Tis very scurvy: and you are —

MOS.   Nay, good sir.

CORV. An arrant locust, by heaven, a locust. Whore,
Crocodile, that hast thy tears prepar'd,
Expecting how thou'lt bid 'em flow.

MOS.   Nay, 'pray you, sir,
She will consider.

CEL.   Would my life would serve   320
To satisfy —

CORV.   'Sdeath! if she would but speak to him,
And save my reputation, 'twere somewhat;
But spitefully to affect my utter ruin!

MOS. [*aside to* CORVINO] Aye, now you have put your fortune
in her hands.
Why, i' faith, it is her modesty, I must quit her;
If you were absent, she would be more coming;

298 *rochet:* a fish (the gurnet).   303 *aqua fortis:* nitric acid.   304 *corsives:* corrosives.   317 *locust:* i.e., a plague.   325 *quit her:* excuse her.

I know it, and dare undertake for her.
What woman can before her husband? 'pray you,
Let us depart and leave her here.

CORV.   Sweet Celia,
Thou may'st redeem all yet; I'll say no more: 330
If not, esteem yourself as lost. Nay, stay there.

[Exit with MOSCA, *shutting the door*

CEL. O God, and his good angels! whither, whither
Is shame fled human breasts? that with such ease
Men dare put off your honours, and their own?
Is that which ever was a cause of life
Now plac'd beneath the basest circumstance,
And modesty an exile made, for money?

VOLP. Aye, in Corvino and such earth-fed minds

[He leaps off from his couch

That never tasted the true heav'n of love.
Assure thee, Celia, he that would sell thee,   340
Only for hope of gain, and that uncertain,
He would have sold his part of Paradise
For ready money, had he met a cope-man.
Why art thou 'maz'd to see me thus reviv'd?
Rather applaud thy beauty's miracle;
'Tis thy great work, that hath, not now alone,
But sundry times, rais'd me in several shapes,
And, but this morning, like a mountebank,
To see thee at thy window. Aye, before
I would have left my practice for thy love,   350
In varying figures I would have contended
With the blue Proteus, or the horned flood.
Now art thou welcome.

CEL.   Sir!

VOLP.   Nay, fly me not.
Nor let thy false imagination
That I was bedrid make thee think I am so:
Thou shalt not find it. I am now as fresh,

343 *cope-man:* merchant, dealer. 350 *practice:* plotting. 351 *varying figures:* different disguises.

As hot, as high, and in as jovial plight,
As when, in that so celebrated scene,
At recitation of our comedy
For entertainment of the great Valois   360
I acted young Antinous; and attracted
The eyes and ears of all the ladies present
T' admire each graceful gesture, note and footing.   [*Sings*

       Come, my Celia, let us prove,
       While we can, the sports of love;
       Time will not be ours for ever,
       He at length our good will sever;
       Spend not then his gifts in vain.
       Suns that set may rise again:
       But if once we lose this light,   370
       'Tis with us perpetual night.
       Why should we defer our joys?
       Fame and rumour are but toys.
       Cannot we delude the eyes
       Of a few poor household spies?
       Or his easier ears beguile,
       Thus removed by our wile?
       'Tis no sin love's fruits to steal;
       But the sweet thefts to reveal:
       To be taken, to be seen,   380
       These have crimes accounted been.

CEL. Some serene blast me, or dire lightning strike
   This my offending face!
VOLP.   Why droops my Celia?
Thou hast in place of a base husband found
A worthy lover: use thy fortune well,
With secrecy and pleasure. See, behold,
What thou art queen of; not in expectation,
As I feed others, but possess'd and crown'd.
See, here, a rope of pearl; and each more orient
Than that the brave Egyptian queen carous'd: 390

382 *serene*: evening mist or dew, which was regarded as harmful.

Dissolve and drink 'em. See, a carbuncle
May put out both the eyes of our St. Mark;
A diamond would have bought Lollia Paulina
When she came in like star-light, hid with jewels
That were the spoils of provinces; take these,
And wear, and lose 'em: yet remains an ear-ring
To purchase them again, and this whole state.
A gem but worth a private patrinomy
Is nothing: we will eat such at a meal.
The heads of parrots, tongues of nightingales,   400
The brains of peacocks and of ostriches
Shall be our food: and, could we get the phœnix,
Though nature lost her kind, she were our dish.
CEL. Good sir, these things might move a mind affected
With such delights; but I, whose innocence
Is all I can think wealthy, or worth th' enjoying,
And which once lost, I have nought to lose beyond it,
Cannot be taken with these sensual baits:
If you have conscience ——
VOLP.   'Tis the beggar's virtue.
If thou hast wisdom, hear me, Celia.   410
Thy baths shall be the juice of July-flowers,
Spirit of roses and of violets,
The milk of unicorns, and panthers' breath
Gather'd in bags and mix'd with Cretan wines.
Our drink shall be prepared gold and amber;
Which we will take until my roof whirl round
With the *vertigo*: and my dwarf shall dance,
My eunuch sing, my fool make up the antic,
Whilst we, in changed shapes, act Ovid's tales,
Thou like Europa now, and I like Jove,   420
Then I like Mars and thou like Erycine;
So of the rest, till we have quite run through

---

391 *carbuncle:* ruby.   403 *though nature lost her kind:* (since there was
only one phoenix at a time, the species would disappear if that one
were eaten).   418 *antic:* dance.   421 *Erycine:* Venus (who was worshipped on Mt. Eryx in Sicily).

And wearied all the fables of the gods.
Then will I have thee in more modern forms,
Attired like some sprightly dame of France,
Brave Tuscan lady, or proud Spanish beauty;
Sometimes unto the Persian Sophie's wife;
Or the Grand Signior's mistress; and for change,
To one of our most artful courtesans,
Or some quick Negro, or cold Russian;
And I will meet thee in as many shapes,   430
Where we may so transfuse our wandering souls
Out at our lips, and score up sums of pleasures,   [*Sings*

       That the curious shall not know,
         How to tell them as they flow;
       And the envious, when they find
         What their number is, be pin'd.

CEL. If you have ears that will be pierc'd; or eyes
   That can be open'd; a heart that may be touch'd;
   Or any part that yet sounds man about you: 440
   If you have touch of holy saints or heaven,
   Do me the grace to let me 'scape. If not,
   Be bountiful and kill me. You do know
   I am a creature hither ill betray'd
   By one whose shame I would forget it were.
   If you will deign me neither of these graces,
   Yet feed your wrath, sir, rather than your lust
   (It is a vice comes nearer manliness,)
   And punish that unhappy crime of nature
   Which you miscall my beauty: flay my face   450
   Or poison it with ointments for seducing
   Your blood to this rebellion. Rub these hands
   With what may cause an eating leprosy
   E'en to my bones and marrow: anything
   That may disfavour me, save in my honour.
   And I will kneel to you, pray for you, pay down

427 *Sophie:* Shah.   428 *Grand Signior:* the Sultan of Turkey.
446 *deign:* grant.

A thousand hourly vows, sir, for your health,
Report, and think you virtuous —

VOLP.   Think me cold,
Frozen, and impotent, and so report me?
That I had Nestor's hernia, thou wouldst think.   460
I do degenerate and abuse my nation
To play with opportunity thus long:
I should have done the act, and then have parley'd.
Yield, or I'll force thee.   [*Seizes her*

CEL.   O! just God.

VOLP.   In vain —
      [BONARIO *leaps out from where* MOSCA *had plac'd him*

BON. Forbear, foul ravisher, libidinous swine!
Free the forc'd lady, or thou diest, impostor.
But that I am loth to snatch thy punishment
Out of the hand of justice, thou shouldst yet
Be made the timely sacrifice of vengeance
Before this altar, and this dross, thy idol.   470
Lady, let's quit the place, it is the den
Of villainy, fear nought, you have a guard:
And he, ere long, shall meet his just reward.
                    [*Exeunt* BONARIO *and* CELIA

VOLP. Fall on me, roof, and bury me in ruin,
Become my grave, that wert my shelter. O!
I am unmask'd, unspirited, undone,
Betray'd to beggary, to infamy —

Enter MOSCA, *wounded*

MOS. Where shall I run, most wretched shame of men,
To beat out my unlucky brains?

VOLP.   Here, here.
What! dost thou bleed?

MOS.   O, that his well-driv'n sword   480
Had been so courteous to have cleft me down
Unto the navel ere I liv'd to see

---

469 *dross:* Volpone's gold plate, etc.   475 *unspirited:* dispirited, dazed.

My life, my hopes, my spirits, my patron, all
  Thus desperately engaged, by my error!
VOLP. Woe on thy fortune!
MOS.   And my follies, sir.
VOLP. Th' hast made me miserable.
MOS.   And myself, sir.
  Who would have thought he would have harken'd so?
VOLP. What shall we do?
MOS.   I know not; if my heart
  Could expiate the mischance, I'd pluck it out.
  Will you be pleas'd to hang me? or cut my throat?   490
  And I'll requite you, sir. Let's die like Romans
  Since we have liv'd like Grecians.   [*They knock without*
VOLP.   Hark, who's there?
  I hear some footing; officers, the *Saffi*,
  Come to apprehend us! I do feel the brand
  Hissing already at my forehead: now
  Mine ears are boring.
MOS.   To your couch, sir. You
  Make that place good, however: [VOLPONE *lies down*
    Guilty men
  Suspect what they deserve still.

Enter CORBACCIO

               Signior Corbaccio!
CORB. Why! how now, Mosca?
MOS.   O, undone, amaz'd, sir.
  Your son, I know not by what accident,   500
  Acquainted with your purpose to my patron
  Touching your will and making him your heir,
  Entered our house with violence, his sword drawn,
  Sought for you, call'd you wretch, unnatural,
  Vow'd he would kill you.

484 *engaged*: involved in danger. 492 *Grecian:* the Greeks were
traditionally 'merry'. 493 *Saffi:* police officers. 494 *brand:* branding
iron. 496–7 *You make the place . . . :* you prove the truth of the saying
that 'Guilty men suspect, etc.'

CORB.   Me?

MOS.   Yes, and my patron.

CORB. This act shall disinherit him indeed:
    Here is the will.

MOS.   'Tis well, sir.

CORB.   Right and well.
    Be you as careful now for me.

Enter VOLTORE, behind

MOS.   My life, sir,
    Is not more tender'd, I am only yours.

CORB. How does he? will he die shortly, think'st thou?   510

MOS.   I fear,
    He'll outlast May.

CORB.   To-day?

MOS.   No, last out May, sir.

CORB. Couldst thou not gi' him a dram?

MOS.   O, by no means, sir.

CORB. Nay, I'll not bid you.

VOLT. [aside]   This is a knave, I see.

MOS. [aside] How, Signior Voltore! did he hear me?

VOLT.   Parasite!

MOS. Who's that? O, sir, most timely welcome —

VOLT.   Scarce
    To the discovery of your tricks, I fear.
    You are his, only? and mine also, are you not?

MOS. Who? I, sir?

VOLT.   You, sir. What device is this
    About a will?

MOS.   A plot for you, sir.

VOLT.   Come,
    Put not your foists upon me, I shall scent 'em.   520

MOS. Did you not hear it?

VOLT.   Yes, I hear Corbaccio
    Hath made your patron there his heir.

MOS.   'Tis true,

       509 *tender'd:* cared for.   520 *foists:* tricks.

By my device, drawn to it by my plot,
With hope —
VOLT.   Your patron should reciprocate?
And you have promis'd?
MOS.   For your good, I did, sir.
Nay, more, I told his son, brought, hid him here,
Where he might hear his father pass the deed;
Being persuaded to it by this thought, sir,
That the unnaturalness, first, of the act,
And then his father's oft disclaiming in him,   530
(Which I did mean t' help on) would sure enrage him
To do some violence upon his parent
On which the law should take sufficient hold,
And you be stated in a double hope:
Truth be my comfort, and my conscience,
My only aim was to dig you a fortune
Out of these two old rotten sepulchres —
VOLT. I cry thee mercy, Mosca.
MOS.   Worth your patience
And your great merit, sir. And see the change!
VOLT. Why? what success?
MOS.   Most hapless! you must help, sir.   540
Whilst we expected the old raven, in comes
Corvino's wife, sent hither by her husband —
VOLT. What, with a present?
MOS.   No, sir, on visitation:
(I'll tell you how, anon) and staying long,
The youth, he grows impatient, rushes forth,
Seizeth the lady, wounds me, makes her swear
(Or he would murder her, that was his vow)
T' affirm my patron to have done her rape:
Which how unlike it is, you see! and hence,
With that pretext, he's gone t' accuse his father,   550
Defame my patron, defeat you —
VOLT.   Where's her husband?
Let him be sent for straight.

                    534 *stated:* established.

MOS.   Sir, I'll go fetch him.

VOLT. Bring him to the *Scrutineo*.

MOS.   Sir, I will.

VOLT. This must be stopp'd.

MOS.   O, you do nobly, sir.
   Alas, 'twas labour'd all, sir, for your good;
   Nor was there want of counsel in the plot:
   But fortune can at any time o'er throw
   The projects of a hundred learned clerks, sir.

CORB. What's that?

VOLT.   Wilt please you, sir, to go along?
                  [*Exit* CORBACCIO, *followed by* VOLTORE

MOS. Patron, go in, and pray for our success.   560

VOLP. [*rising from his couch*] Need makes devotion: heaven your
   labour bless.   [*Exeunt*

       553 *the Scrutineo:* the Senate House of Venice.

ACT IV

Scene I

[*A street*]
Enter SIR POLITIC WOULD-BE *and* PEREGRINE

POL. I told you, sir, it was a plot: you see
   What observation is. You mention'd me
   For some instructions: I will tell you, sir,
   (Since we are met here in this height of Venice)
   Some few particulars I have set down,
   Only for this meridian, fit to be known
   Of your crude traveller, and they are these.
   I will not touch, sir, at your phrase or clothes,
   For they are old.
PER.   Sir, I have better.
POL.   Pardon,
   I meant, as they are themes.
PER.   O, sir, proceed: 10
   I'll slander you no more of wit, good sir.
POL. First, for your garb, it must be grave and serious;
   Very reserv'd and lock'd; not tell a secret
   On any terms, not to your father; scarce
   A fable, but with caution; make sure choice
   Both of your company and discourse; beware
   You never speak a truth —
PER.   How!
POL.   Not to strangers,
   For those be they you must converse with most;
   Others I would not know, sir, but at distance,
   So as I still might be a saver in 'em: 20
   You shall have tricks, else, pass'd upon you hourly.

2 *mention'd:* asked.   10 *themes:* subjects for discussion.   12 *garb:*
outward appearance and behaviour.   13 *lock'd:* reticent.

G   81

And then, for your religion, profess none,
But wonder at the diversity of all;
And, for your part, protest, were there no other
But simply the laws o' th' land, you could content you:
Nic. Machiavel and Monsieur Bodin, both
Were of this mind. Then must you learn the use
And handling of your silver fork at meals;
The metal of your glass (these are main matters
With your Italian): and to know the hour   30
When you must eat your melons and your figs.
PER. Is that a point of state too?
POL.   Here it is.
For your Venetian, if he see a man
Preposterous in the least, he has him straight;
He has: he strips him. I'll acquaint you, sir,
I now have liv'd here, 'tis some fourteen months;
Within the first week of my landing here
All took me for a citizen of Venice,
I knew the forms so well —
PER. [aside]   And nothing else.
POL. I had read Contarene, took me a house,   40
Dealt with my Jews to furnish it with movables —
Well, if I could but find one man, one man,
To mine own heart, whom I durst trust, I would —
PER. What? What, sir?
POL.   Make him rich; make him a fortune:
He should not think again. I would command it.
PER. As how?
POL.   With certain projects that I have,
Which I may not discover.
PER. [aside]   If I had
But one to wager with, I would lay odds now,
He tells me instantly.
POL.   One is (and that
I care not greatly who knows) to serve the state   50
Of Venice with red herrings for three years,

25 *Content you:* be content.

And at a certain rate, from Rotterdam,
Where I have correspondence. There's a letter,
Sent me from one o' the States, and to that purpose;
He cannot write his name, but that's his mark.
PER. He is a chandler?
POL.   No, a cheesemonger.
There are some others too, with whom I treat
About the same negotiation;
And I will undertake it: for, 'tis thus —
I'll do 't with ease, I have cast it all. Your hoy   60
Carries but three men in her, and a boy,
And she shall make me three returns a year:
So, if there come but one of three, I save;
If two, I can defalk. But this is now,
If my main project fail.
PER.   Then you have others?
POL. I should be loth to draw the subtle air
Of such a place without my thousand aims.
I'll not dissemble, sir, where'er I come
I love to be considerative; and 'tis true
I have at my free hours thought upon   70
Some certain goods unto the state of Venice,
Which I do call my cautions: and, sir, which
I mean, in hope of pension, to propound
To the Great Council, then unto the Forty,
So to the Ten. My means are made already —
PER. By whom?
POL.   Sir, one that though his place be obscure,
Yet he can sway, and they will hear him. He's
A *commandadore*.
PER.   What, a common sergeant?
POL. Sir, such as they are, put it in their mouths
What they should say, sometimes, as well as greater.   80

53 *correspondence:* contacts.   54 *the States:* i.e., of the Netherlands.
56 *chandler:* grocer. 60 *cast:* reckoned it out. *hoy:* a small ship.
64 *defalk:* reduce the amount.   69 *considerative:* thoughtful.
72 *cautions:* precautions.

I think I have my notes to show you —
PER.   Good, sir.
POL. But you shall swear unto me, on your gentry,
    Not to anticipate —
PER.   I, sir?
POL.   Nor reveal
    A circumstance — My paper is not with me.
PER. O, but you can remember, sir.
POL.   My first is
    Concerning tinder-boxes. You must know,
    No family is here without its box.
    Now, sir, it being so portable a thing,
    Put case that you or I were ill affected
    Unto the state; sir, with it in our pockets,   90
    Might not I go into the Arsenal,
    Or you, come out again, and none the wiser?
PER. Except yourself, sir.
POL.   Go to, then. I therefore
    Advertise to the state how fit it were
    That none but such as were known patriots,
    Sound lovers of their country, should be suffer'd
    T' enjoy them in their houses: and even those
    Seal'd at some office, and at such a bigness
    As might not lurk in pockets.
PER.   Admirable!
POL. My next is, how t' inquire and be resolv'd   100
    By present demonstration, whether a ship
    Newly arrived from Syria, or from
    Any suspected part of all the Levant,
    Be guilty of the plague: and where they use
    To lie out forty, fifty days, sometimes,
    About the Lazaretto for their trial,
    I'll save that charge and loss unto the merchant,
    And, in an hour, clear the doubt.
PER.   Indeed, sir?

89 *put case*: suppose. 89 *ill affected*: hostile to. 101 *present demon-
stration*: immediate proof. 106 *Lazaretto*: pest-house, quarantine.

POL. Or — I will lose my labour.

PER.   'My faith, that's much.

POL. Nay, sir, conceive me. 'Twill cost me in onions   110
  Some thirty livres —

PER.   Which is one pound sterling.

POL. Beside my waterworks : for this I do, sir.
  First, I bring in your ship 'twixt two brick walls
  (But those the state shall venture); on the one
  I strain me a fair tarpaulin, and in that
  I stick my onions, cut in halves : the other
  Is full of loop-holes, out at which I thrust
  The noses of my bellows; and those bellows
  I keep, with waterworks, in perpetual motion,
  Which is the easiest matter of a hundred.   120
  Now, sir, your onion, which doth naturally
  Attract th' infection, and your bellows blowing
  The air upon him, will show instantly,
  By his chang'd colour, if there be contagion,
  Or else remain as fair as at the first.
  Now 'tis known, 'tis nothing.

PER.   You are right, sir.

POL. I would I had my note.

PER.   'Faith, so would I:
  But you ha' done well for once, sir.

POL.   Were I false,
  Or would be made so, I could show you reasons
  How I could sell this state now to the Turk,   130
  Spite of their galleys, or their —   [examining his papers

PER.   Pray you, Sir Pol.

POL. I have 'em not about me.

PER.   That I fear'd.
  They are there, sir?

POL.   No, this is my diary
  Wherein I note my actions of the day.

PER. 'Pray you let's see, sir. What is here? *notandum*,   [Reads

112 *Waterworks:* hydraulic device.   114 *venture:* pay for.   115 *strain
me:* stretch.

'A rat had gnawn my spur-leathers; notwithstanding,
I put on new and did go forth: but first
I threw three beans over the threshold. *Item*,
I went and bought two toothpicks, whereof one
I burst immediately, in a discourse   140
With a Dutch merchant, 'bout *ragion del stato*.
From him I went, and paid a *moccinigo*
For piecing my silk stockings; by the way
I cheapen'd sprats: and at St. Mark's, I urin'd.'
'Faith, these are politic notes!

POL.   Sir, I do slip
No action of my life, thus, but I quote it.

PER. Believe me, it is wise!

POL.   Nay, sir, read forth.

Enter LADY POLITIC WOULD-BE, NANO, *and two*
WAITING-WOMEN

LADY P. Where should this loose knight be, trow? sure he's
    hous'd.

NAN. Why, then he's fast.

LADY P.   Aye, he plays both with me.
I pray you, stay. This heat will do more harm   150
To my complexion than his heart is worth.
I do not care to hinder, but to take him.
How it comes off!   [*Rubbing her cheeks*

WOM.   My master's yonder.

LADY P.   Where?

WOM. With a young gentleman.

LADY P.   That same's the party,
In man's apparel! 'Pray you, sir, jog my knight:
I will be tender to his reputation,
However he demerit.

POL.   My lady!

PER.   Where?

141 *ragion del stato:* politics.   143 *piecing:* mending.   144 *cheapen'd:*
bargained for.   145 *slip:* let go by.   157 *However he demerit:* however
little he deserves it.

POL. 'Tis she indeed, sir; you shall know her. She is,
   Were she not mine, a lady of that merit,
   For fashion and behaviour, and for beauty,   160
   I durst compare —
PER.   It seems you are not jealous,
   That dare commend her.
POL.   Nay, and for discourse —
PER. Being your wife, she cannot miss that.
POL.   Madam,
   Here is a gentleman, 'pray you use him fairly.
   He seems a youth, but he is —
LADY P.   None?
POL.   Yes, one
   Has put his face as soon into the world —
LADY P. You mean, as early? But to-day?
POL.   How's this!
LADY P. Why, in this habit, sir, you apprehend me.
   Well, Master Would-be, this doth not become you;
   I had thought the odour, sir, of your good name   170
   Had been more precious to you; that you would not
   Have done this dire massacre on your honour;
   One of your gravity and rank besides!
   But knights, I see, care little for the oath
   They make to ladies; chiefly their own ladies.
POL. Now, by my spurs, the symbol of my knighthood!
PER. [aside] Lord! how his brain is humbled for an oath.
POL. I reach you not.
LADY P.   Right, sir, your policy
   May bear it through thus. [To PEREGRINE] Sir, a word with
      you.
   I would be loth to contest publicly   180
   With any gentlewoman, or to seem
   Froward, or violent, as the courtier says;
   It comes too near rusticity in a lady,
   Which I would shun by all means: and, however

166 *Has put his face . . . world:* has made his entry thus early into life.
178 *reach you not:* don't understand your meaning. *policy:* craftiness.

I may deserve from Master Would-be, yet
T' have one fair gentlewoman thus be made
Th' unkind instrument to wrong another,
And one she knows not, aye, and to persever,
In my poor judgement is not warranted
From being a solecism in our sex,   190
If not in manners.

PER.   How is this!
POL.   Sweet madam,
Come nearer to your aim.
LADY P.   Marry, and will, sir.
Since you provoke me with your impudence,
And laughter of your light land-siren here,
Your Sporus, your hermaphrodite —
PER.   What's here?
Poetic fury and historic storms!
POL. The gentleman, believe it, is of worth,
And of our nation.
LADY P.   Aye, your Whitefriars nation.
Come, I blush for you, Master Would-be, aye;
And am asham'd you should ha' no more forehead   200
Than thus to be the patron or St. George
To a lewd harlot, a base fricatrice,
A female devil in a male outside.
POL.   Nay,
An you be such a one, I must bid adieu
To your delights. The case appears too liquid.   [Exit
LADY P. Aye, you may carry 't clear with your state-face!
But for your carnival concupiscence,
Who here is fled for liberty of conscience,
From furious persecution of the marshal,

183 *rusticity:* bad breeding.   189-90 *warranted from ... solecism:*
must be regarded as a serious lapse. 200 *forehead:* sense of shame.
202 *fricatrice:* prostitute. 204 *An:* if. 205 *liquid:* clear (and perhaps
Lady Politic Would-be is crying). 206 *state-face:* composed counten-
ance. 207 *carnival concupiscence:* (cf. the modern 'good-time girl' —
but Lady Politic Would-be is probably confusing 'carnival', as de-
scribing an occasion of general licence, and 'carnal'). 209 *marshal:*
prison officer.

    Her will I disc'ple.

PER.   This is fine, i' faith!   210
    And do you use this often? Is this part
    Of your wit's exercise, 'gainst you have occasion?
    Madam —

LADY P.   Go to, sir.

PER.   Do you hear me, lady?
    Why, if your knight have set you to beg shirts,
    Or to invite me home, you might have done it
    A nearer way by far.

LADY P.   This cannot work you
    Out of my snare.

PER.   Why, am I in it then?
    Indeed, your husband told me you were fair,
    And so you are; only your nose inclines,
    That side that's next the sun, to the queen-apple.   220

LADY P. This cannot be endur'd by any patience.

Enter MOSCA

MOS. What's the matter, madam?

LADY P.   If the Senate
    Right not my quest in this, I will protest 'em,
    To all the world, no aristocracy.

MOS. What is the injury, lady?

LADY P.   Why, the callet
    You told me of, here I have ta'en disguis'd.

MOS. Who? this? what means your ladyship? the creature
    I mention'd to you is apprehended now,
    Before the Senate, you shall see her —

LADY P.   Where?

MOS. I'll bring you to her. This young gentleman,   230
    I saw him land this morning at the port.

LADY P. Is 't possible! How has my judgement wander'd!
    Sir, I must, blushing, say to you I have err'd

210 *disc'ple:* discipline, punish.   219–20 *inclines . . . queen-apple:* is red, like an apple which ripens on the side that gets most sunshine. 223 *quest:* case, complaint. *protest:* proclaim. 225 *callet:* bad girl.

And plead your pardon.

PER.   What! more changes yet?

LADY P. I hope yo' ha' not the malice to remember
    A gentlewoman's passion. If you stay
    In Venice here, please to use me, sir —

MOS. Will you go, madam?

LADY P.   'Pray you, sir, use me. In faith,
    The more you see me, the more I shall conceive
    You have forgot our quarrel   [*Exeunt all but* PEREGRINE

PER.   This is rare!   240
    Sir Politic Would-be? no, Sir Politic bawd,
    To bring me thus acquainted with his wife!
    Well, wise Sir Pol., since you have practis'd thus
    Upon my freshman-ship, I'll try your salt-head,
    What proof it is against a counter-plot.   [*Exit*

Scene II

[*The Senate House*]
Enter VOLTORE, CORBACCIO, CORVINO, *and* MOSCA

VOLT. Well, now you know the carriage of the business,
    Your constancy is all that is requir'd
    Unto the safety of it.   [*He stands aside*

MOS.   Is the lie
    Safely convey'd amongst us? is that sure?
    Knows every man his burden?

CORV.   Yes.

MOS.   Then shrink not.

CORV. But knows the Advocate the truth?

MOS.   O, sir,
    By no means. I devis'd a formal tale

239 *conceive:* believe, understand (but Peregrine takes it the wrong
way). 243 *practis'd:* played tricks. 244 *salt-head:* old (as opposed
to 'fresh'), and possibly lecherous as well.   1 *carriage:* conduct.
4 *convey'd:* agreed, settled. 5 *burden:* his part in the chorus, what he
has to say.

That salv'd your reputation. But be valiant, sir.

CORV. I fear no one but him; that this his pleading
   Should make him stand for a co-heir —

MOS.   Co-halter!   10
   Hang him: we will but use his tongue, his noise,
   As we do croaker's, here.

CORV.   Aye, what shall he do?

MOS. When we ha' done, you mean?

CORV.   Yes.

MOS.   Why, we'll think:
   Sell him for *mummia*, he's half dust already.
   Do not you smile [*to* VOLTORE] to see this buffalo,
   How he doth sport it with his head? — [*aside*] I should,
   If all were well and past. Sir [*to* CORBACCIO], only you
   Are he that shall enjoy the crop of all,
   And these not know for whom they toil.

CORB.   Aye, peace.

MOS. [*to* CORVINO, *then to* VOLTORE *again*] But you shall eat
   it. Much! Worshipful sir,   20
   Mercury sit upon you thundering tongue,
   Or the French Hercules, and make your language
   As conquering as his club, to beat along,
   As with a tempest, flat, our adversaries:
   But much more yours, sir.

VOLT.   Here they come, ha' done.

MOS. I have another witness, if you need, sir,
   I can produce.

VOLT.   Who is it?

MOS.   Sir, I have her.

   Enter AVOCATORI, BONARIO, CELIA, NOTARIO,
   COMMANDADORI, *and other* OFFICERS OF JUSTICE

1 AVOC. The like of this the Senate never heard of.

2 AVOC. 'Twill come most strange to them when we report it.

8 *salv'd:* protected.   10 *co-heir:* i.e., of Volpone.   12 *croaker's:*
Corbaccio's.   14 *mummia:* a drug, said to be made from Egyptian
mummies.

4 AVOC. The gentlewoman has been ever held 30
Of unreproved name.

3 AVOC. So the young man.

4 AVOC. The more unnatural part that of his father.

2 AVOC. More of the husband.

1 AVOC. I not know to give
His act a name, it is so monstrous!

4 AVOC. But the impostor, he is a thing created
T' exceed example!

1 AVOC. And all after-times!

2 AVOC. I never heard a true voluptuary
Describ'd, but him.

3 AVOC. Appear yet those were cited?

NOT. All but the old magnifico, Volpone.

1 AVOC. Why is not he here?

MOS. Please your fatherhoods, 40
Here is his advocate. Himself's so weak,
So feeble —

4 AVOC. What are you?

BON. His parasite,
His knave, his pandar: I beseech the court
He may be forc'd to come, that your grave eyes
May bear strong witness of his strange impostures.

VOLT. Upon my faith and credit with your virtues,
He is not able to endure the air.

2 AVOC. Bring him, however.

3 AVOC. We will see him.

4 AVOC. Fetch him.

VOLT. Your fatherhoods' fit pleasures be obey'd,

[*Exeunt* OFFICERS

But sure, the sight will rather move your pities 50
Than indignation; may it please the court,
In the meantime, he may be heard in me:
I know this place most void of prejudice,
And therefore crave it, since we have no reason

31 *unreproved name:* unspotted reputation. 37 *voluptuary:* debauched person.

To fear our truth should hurt our cause.

3 AVOC.   Speak free.

VOLT. Then know, most honour'd fathers, I must now
Discover to your strangely abused ears
The most prodigious and most frontless piece
Of solid impudence and treachery
That ever vicious nature yet brought forth   60
To shame the state of Venice. This lewd woman,
That wants no artificial looks or tears
To help the visor she has now put on,
Hath long been known a close adulteress
To that lascivious youth there; not suspected,
I say, but known, and taken in the act
With him; and by this man, the easy husband,
Pardon'd; whose timeless bounty makes him now
Stand here, the most unhappy innocent person
That ever man's own goodness made accus'd.   70
For these, not knowing how to owe a gift
Of that dear grace but with their shame; being plac'd
So above all powers of their gratitude,
Began to hate the benefit: and, in place
Of thanks, devise t' extirp the memory
Of such an act. Wherein I pray your fatherhoods
To observe the malice, yea, the rage of creatures
Discover'd in their evils; and what heart
Such take, even from their crimes. But that anon
Will more appear. This gentleman, the father,   80
Hearing of this foul fact, with many others
Which daily struck at his too tender ears,
And griev'd in nothing more than that he could not
Preserve himself a parent (his son's ills
Growing to that strange flood), at last decreed
To disinherit him.

1 AVOC.   These be strange turns!

2 AVOC. The young man's fame was ever fair and honest.

58 *frontless*: shameless.   62 *wants:* lacks.   64 *close:* secret.   68 *time-less:* untimely.   71 *owe:* accept.   75 *extirp:* wipe out.

VOLT. So much more full of danger is his vice,
   That can beguile so under shade of virtue.
   But as I said, my honour'd sires, his father,   90
   Having this settled purpose, by what means
   To him betray'd we know not, and this day
   Appointed for the deed; that parricide
   (I cannot style him better), by confederacy
   Preparing this his paramour to be there,
   Entered Volpone's house, who was the man,
   Your fatherhoods must understand, design'd
   For the inheritance, there sought his father:
   But with what purpose sought he him, my lords?
   I tremble to pronounce it, that a son   100
   Unto a father, and to such a father,
   Should have so foul, felonious intent —
   It was to murder him. When, being prevented
   By his more happy absence, what then did he?
   Not check his wicked thoughts; no, now new deeds
   (Mischief doth never end where it begins);
   An act of horror, fathers! he dragg'd forth
   The aged gentleman that had there lain bed-rid
   Three years and more, out of his innocent couch,
   Naked upon the floor there left him; wounded   110
   His servant in the face; and with this strumpet,
   The stale to his forg'd practice, who was glad
   To be so active (I shall here desire
   Your fatherhoods to note but my collections,
   As most remarkable), thought at once to stop
   His father's ends; discredit his free choice
   In the old gentleman: redeem themselves
   By laying infamy upon this man,
   To whom, with blushing, they should owe their lives.
1 AVOC. What proofs have you of this?
BON.   Most honour'd fathers, 120
   I humbly crave there be no credit given

112 *stale:* decoy. *forg'd practice:* criminal deceit. 114 *collections:* evidence.

To this man's mercenary tongue.

2 AVOC.   Forbear.

BON. His soul moves in his fee.

3 AVOC.   O, sir.

BON.   This fellow,
For six sols more, would plead against his Maker.

1 AVOC. You do forget yourself.

VOLT.   Nay, nay, grave fathers,
Let him have scope: can any man imagine
That he will spare his accuser that would not
Have spar'd his parent?

1 AVOC.   Well, produce your proofs.

CEL. I would I could forget I were a creature.

VOLT. Signior Corbaccio.   [CORBACCIO *comes forward*

4 AVOC.   What is he?

VOLT.   The father.   130

2 AVOC. Has he had an oath?

NOT.   Yes.

CORB.   What must I do now?

NOT. Your testimony's crav'd.

CORB.   Speak to the knave?
I'll ha' my mouth first stopp'd with earth; my heart
Abhors his knowledge: I disclaim in him.

1 AVOC. But for what cause?

CORB.   The mere portent of nature.
He is an utter stranger to my loins.

BON. Have they made you to this?

CORB.   I will not hear thee,
Monster of men, swine, goat, wolf, parricide,
Speak not, thou viper.

BON.   Sir, I will sit down,
And rather wish my innocence should suffer   140
Than I resist the authority of a father.

VOLT. Signior Corvino.   [CORVINO *comes forward*

2 AVOC.   This is strange!

124 *sol:* small coin, worth about ½d.   134 *disclaim in him:* disclaim any
share in him.   135 *portent:* monster, prodigy.

1 AVOC.   Who's this?

NOT. The husband.

4 AVOC.   Is he sworn?

NOT.   He is.

3 AVOC.   Speak then.

CORV. This woman, please your fatherhoods, is a whore,
    Of most hot exercise, more than a partidge,
    Upon record —

1 AVOC.   No more.

CORV.   Neighs like a jennet.

NOT. Preserve the honour of the court.

CORV.   I shall,
    And modesty of your most reverend ears.
    And yet I hope that I may say these eyes
    Have seen her glued unto that piece of cedar,   150
    That fine well-timber'd gallant: and that here
    The letters may be read, thorough the horn,
    That make the story perfect.

MOS. [aside]   Excellent, sir!

CORV. [aside] There is no shame in this now, is there?

MOS. [aside]   None.

CORV. Or if I said I hop'd that she were onward
    To her damnation, if there be a hell
    Greater than whore and woman; a good Catholic
    May make the doubt.

3 AVOC.   His grief hath made him frantic.

1 AVOC. Remove him hence.

2 AVOC.   Look to the woman.   [CELIA swoons

CORV.   Rare!
    Prettily feign'd again!

4 AVOC.   Stand from about her.   160

1 AVOC. Give her the air.

3 AVOC [to MOSCA]   What can you say?

MOS.   My wound,
    May 't please your wisdoms, speaks for me, receiv'd
    In aid of my good patron, when he missed

        145 exercise: behaviour.   146 jennet: a young mare.

His sought-for father, when that well-taught dame
Had her cue given her to cry out a rape.

BON. O, most laid impudence! Fathers —

3 AVOC.   Sir, be silent.
You had your hearing free, so must they theirs.

2 AVOC. I do begin to doubt th' imposture here.

4 AVOC. This woman has too many moods.

VOLT.   Grave fathers,
She is a creature of a most profess'd   170
And prostituted lewdness.

CORV.   Most impetuous!
Unsatisfied, grave fathers!

VOLT.   May her feignings
Not take your wisdoms: but this day she baited
A stranger, a grave knight, with her loose eyes
And more lascivious kisses. This man saw 'em
Together on the water in a gondola.

MOS. Here is the lady herself, that saw 'em too,
Without; who then had in the open streets
Pursu'd them, but for saving her knight's honour.

1 AVOC. Produce that lady.   [Exit MOSCA

2 AVOC.   Let her come.

4 AVOC.   These things,   180
They strike with wonder!

3 AVOC.   I am turn'd a stone!

Re-enter MOSCA *with* LADY POLITIC WOULD-BE

MOS. Be resolute, madam.

LADY P. [*pointing to* CELIA] Aye, this same is she.
Out, thou chameleon harlot; now thine eyes
Vie tears with the hyena: dar'st thou look
Upon my wronged face? I cry your pardons.
I fear I have forgettingly transgress'd
Against the dignity of the court —

2 AVOC.   No, madam.

166 *laid:* carefully planned.   173 *but this day:* this very day.   *baited:*
tempted.

H

LADY P. And been exorbitant —

4 AVOC.   You have not, lady.
These proofs are strong.

LADY P.   Surely, I had no purpose
To scandalize your honours, or my sex's.   190

3 AVOC. We do believe it.

LADY P.   Surely, you may believe it.

2 AVOC. Madam, we do.

LADY P.   Indeed, you may; my breeding
Is not so coarse —

4 AVOC.   We know it.

LADY P.   To offend
With pertinacy —

3 AVOC.   Lady.

LADY P.   Such a presence:
No, surely.

I AVOC. We well think it.

LADY P.   You may think it.

I AVOC. Let her o'ercome. What witnesses have you
To make good your report?

BON.   Our consciences.

CEL. And heaven, that never fails the innocent.

4 AVOC. These are no testimonies.

BON.   Not in your courts,
Where multitude and clamour overcomes.   200

I AVOC. Nay, then you do wax insolent.

                    [VOLPONE *is brought in on a couch*

VOLT.   Here, here,
The testimony comes that will convince,
And put to utter dumbness their bold tongues.
See here, grave fathers, here's the ravisher,
The rider on men's wives, the great impostor,
The grand voluptuary! Do you not think
These limbs should affect venery? or these eyes
Covet a concubine? 'pray you mark these hands.
Are they not fit to stroke a lady's breasts?

          207 *venery:* lechery.

    Perhaps he doth dissemble?

BON.   So he does.   210

VOLT. Would you ha' him tortur'd?

BON.   I would have him prov'd.

VOLT. Best try him then, with goads or burning irons;
    Put him to the strappado: I have heard
    The rack hath cur'd the gout; faith, give it him,
    And help him of a malady, be courteous.
    I'll undertake, before these honour'd fathers,
    He shall have yet as many left diseases
    As she has known adulterers, or thou strumpets.
    O, my most equal hearers, if these deeds,
    Acts of this bold and most exorbitant strain,   220
    May pass with sufferance, what one citizen
    But owes the forfeit of his life, yea, fame,
    To him that dares traduce him? which of you
    Are safe, my honour'd fathers? I would ask,
    With leave of your grave fatherhoods, if their plot
    Have any face or colour like to truth?
    Or if, unto the dullest nostril here,
    It smell not rank and most abhorred slander?
    I crave your care of this good gentleman,
    Whose life is much endanger'd by their fable;   230
    And as for them, I will conclude with this,
    That vicious persons, when they are hot and flesh'd
    In impious acts, their constancy abounds:
    Damn'd deeds are done with greatest confidence.

1 AVOC. Take 'em to custody, and sever them.

2 AVOC. 'Tis pity two such prodigies should live.

1 AVOC. Let the old gentleman be return'd with care:
    I am sorry our credulity wrong'd him.

                           [VOLPONE *is carried out*

4 AVOC. These are two creatures!

3 AVOC.   I have an earthquake in me!

---

213 *strappado:* a form of torture, in which the victim was hauled up and down a rope. 232 *flesh'd:* experienced. 233 *constancy:* persistence. 235 *sever:* separate.

2 AVOC. Their shame, even in their cradles, fled their
    faces.   240
4 AVOC. [to VOLTORE] You have done a worthy service to the
    state, sir,
    In their discovery.
1 AVOC.   You shall hear ere night
    What punishment the court decrees upon 'em.
        [Exeunt AVOCATORI, NOTARIO, and OFFICERS with
        BONARIO and CELIA
VOLT. We thank your fatherhoods. How like you it?
MOS.   Rare.
    I'd ha' your tongue, sir, tipp'd with gold, for this;
    I'd ha' you be the heir to the whole city;
    The earth I'd have want men, ere you want living:
    They are bound to erect your statue in St. Mark's.
    Signior Corvino, I would have you go
    And show yourself, that you have conquer'd.
CORV.   Yes.   250
MOS. It was much better that you should profess
    Yourself a cuckold, thus, than that the other
    Should have been prov'd.
CORV.   Nay, I consider'd that:
    Now it is her fault.
MOS.   Then it had been yours.
CORV. True. I do doubt this advocate still.
MOS.   I' faith,
    You need not. I dare ease you of that care.
CORV. I trust thee, Mosca.   [Exit
MOS.   As your own soul, sir.
CORB.   Mosca!
MOS. Now for your business, sir.
CORB.   How? ha' you business?
MOS. Yes, yours, sir.
CORB.   O, none else?
MOS.   None else, not I.
CORB. Be careful then.
MOS.   Rest you with both your eyes, sir.   260

CORB. Dispatch it.

MOS.   Instantly.

CORB.   And look that all
Whatever be put in, jewels, plate, moneys,
Household stuff, bedding, curtains —

MOS.   Curtain rings, sir;
Only, the advocate's fee must be deducted.

CORB. I'll pay him now: you'll be too prodigal.

MOS. Sir, I must tender it.

CORB.   Two *cecchines* is well?

MOS. No, six, sir.

CORB.   'Tis too much.

MOS.   He talk'd a great while;
You must consider that, sir.

CORB.   Well, there's three —

MOS. I'll give it him.

CORB.   Do so, and there's for thee.   [*Exit*

MOS. Bountiful bones! What horrid strange offence   270
Did he commit 'gainst nature, in his youth,
Worthy this age? [*Aside*] You see, sir, how I work
Unto your ends; take you no notice.

VOLT.   No,
I'll leave you.   [*Exit*

MOS.   All is yours, the devil and all,
Good advocate. Madam, I'll bring you home.

LADY P. No, I'll go see your patron.

MOS.   That you shall not:
I'll tell you why. My purpose is to urge
My patron to reform his will; and for
The zeal you have shown to-day, whereas before
You were but third or fourth, you shall be now   280
Put in the first: which would appear as begged
If you were present. Therefore —

LADY P.   You shall sway me.   [*Exeunt*

ACT V

Scene I

[VOLPONE's *house*]
Enter VOLPONE

VOLP. Well, I am here; and all this brunt is past:
   I ne'er was in dislike with my disguise
   Till this fled moment; here 'twas good, in private,
   But, in your public, *cave*, whilst I breathe.
   'Fore God, my left leg 'gan to have the cramp,
   And I apprehended straight some power had struck me
   With a dead palsy: well, I must be merry,
   And shake it off. A many of these fears
   Would put me into some villainous disease,
   Should they come thick upon me: I'll prevent 'em.   10
   Give me a bowl of lusty wine to fright
   This humour from my heart; [*he drinks*] hum, hum, hum!
   'Tis almost gone already: I shall conquer.
   Any device now, of rare, ingenious knavery,
   That would possess me with a violent laughter,
   Would wake me up again! [*Drinks again*] So, so, so, so.
   This heat is life; 'tis blood by this time: Mosca!

Enter MOSCA

MOS. How now, sir? does the day look clear again?
   Are we recover'd, and wrought out of error,
   Into our way, to see our path before us?   20
   Is our trade free once more?
VOLP.   Exquisite Mosca!
MOS. Was it not carried learnedly?
VOLP.   And stoutly.

    1 *brunt:* crisis.   6 *apprehended:* feared.

Good wits are greatest in extremities.

MOS. It were a folly beyond thought to trust
Any grand act unto a cowardly spirit:
You are not taken with it enough, methinks?

VOLP. O, more than if I had enjoy'd the wench:
The pleasure of all womankind's not like it.

MOS. Why, now you speak, sir. We must here be fix'd;
Here we must rest; this is our masterpiece: 30
We cannot think to go beyond this.

VOLP.   True,
Thou hast play'd thy prize, my precious Mosca.

MOS.   Nay, sir,
To gull the court —

VOLP.   And quite divert the torrent
Upon the innocent.

MOS.   Yes, and to make
So rare a music out of discords —

VOLP.   Right.
That yet to me 's the strangest! How th' hast borne it!
That these, being so divided 'mongst themselves,
Should not scent somewhat, or in me or thee,
Or doubt their own side.

MOS.   True, they will not see 't.
Too much light blinds 'em, I think. Each of 'em   40
Is so possess'd and stuff'd with his own hopes
That anything unto the contrary,
Never so true, or never so apparent,
Never so palpable, they will resist it —

VOLP. Like a temptation of the devil.

MOS.   Right, sir.
Merchants may talk of trade, and your great signiors
Of land that yields well; but if Italy
Have any glebe more fruitful than these fellows,
I am deceiv'd. Did not your advocate rare?

VOLP. O — 'My most honour'd fathers, my grave fathers,   50

32 *play'd thy prize:* produced your masterpiece.   48 *glebe:* soil, land.

Under correction of your fatherhoods,
What face of truth is here? If these strange deeds
May pass, most honour'd fathers' — I had much ado
To forbear laughing.

MOS.   'T seem'd to me you sweat, sir.

VOLP. In troth, I did a little.

MOS.   But confess, sir,
Were you not daunted?

VOLP.   In good faith, I was
A little in a mist; but not dejected:
Never, but still myself.

MOS.   I think it, sir.
Now, so truth help me, I must needs say this, sir,
And out of conscience, for your advocate: 60
He has taken pains, in faith, sir, and deserv'd,
In my poor judgement, I speak it under favour,
Not to contrary you, sir, very richly —
Well — to be cozen'd.

VOLP.   'Troth, and I think so too,
By that I heard him in the latter end.

MOS. O, but before, sir; had you heard him first
Draw it to certain heads, then aggravate,
Then use his vehement figures — I look'd still
When he would shift a shirt; and doing this
Out of pure love, no hope of gain —

VOLP.   'Tis right.   70
I cannot answer him, Mosca, as I would,
Not yet; but for thy sake, at thy entreaty,
I will begin, ev'n now, to vex 'em all:
This very instant.

MOS.   Good, sir.

VOLP.   Call the dwarf
And eunuch forth.

63 *contrary:* contradict. 64 *cozen'd:* tricked. 65 *in the latter end:* in
the last part of his speech. 67 *Draw . . . heads:* make certain points.
aggravate: emphasize. 68 *vehement figures:* violent metaphors. 69 *shift
a shirt:* change his shirt (because his violent gestures had made him
sweat).

MOS.   Castrone, Nano!

Enter CASTRONE *and* NANO

NAN.   Here.
VOLP. Shall we have a jig now?
MOS.   What you please, sir.
VOLP.   Go,
   Straight give out about the streets, you two,
   That I am dead; do it with constancy,
   Sadly, do you hear? impute it to the grief
   Of this late slander.   [*Exeunt* CASTRONE *and* NANO
MOS.   What do you mean, sir?
VOLP.   O,   80
   I shall have instantly my vulture, crow,
   Raven, come flying hither on the news,
   To peck for carrion, my she-wolf, and all
   Greedy, and full of expectation —
MOS. And then to have it ravish'd from their mouths?
VOLP. 'Tis true; I will ha' thee put on a gown,
   And take upon thee as thou wert mine heir;
   Show 'em a will: open that chest, and reach
   Forth one of those that has the blanks. I'll straight
   Put in thy name.
MOS.   It will be rare, sir.
VOLP.   Aye,   90
   When they e'en gape, and find themselves deluded —
MOS. Yes.
VOLP.   And thou use them scurvily. Dispatch,
   Get on thy gown.
MOS. [*putting on a gown*] But what, sir, if they ask
   After the body?
VOLP.   Say it was corrupted.
MOS. I'll say it stunk, sir; and was fain t' have it
   Coffin'd up instantly, and sent away.
VOLP. Anything, what thou wilt. Hold, here's my will.

79 *sadly:* soberly.

Get thee a cap, a count-book, pen and ink,
Papers afore thee; sit as thou wert taking
An inventory of parcels: I'll get up,   100
Behind the curtain, on a stool, and hearken;
Sometime peep over; see how they do look;
With what degrees their blood doth leave their faces!
O, 'twill afford me a rare meal of laughter.
MOS. Your advocate will turn stark dull upon it.
VOLP. It will take off his oratory's edge.
MOS. But your *clarissimo*, old round-back, he
   Will crump you like a hog-louse with the touch.
VOLP. And what Corvino?
MOS.   O, sir, look for him,
   To-morrow morning, with a rope and dagger,   110
   To visit all the streets; he must run mad.
   My lady too, that came into the court
   To bear false witness for your worship —
VOLP.   Yes,
   And kiss'd me 'fore the fathers, when my face
   Flow'd all with oils.
MOS.   And sweat, sir. Why, your gold
   Is such another med'cine, it dries up
   All those offensive savours! It transforms
   The most deformed, and restores 'em lovely,
   As 't were the strange poetical girdle. Jove
   Could not invent t' himself a shroud more subtle   120
   To pass Acrisius' guards. It is the thing
   Makes all the world her grace, her youth, her beauty.
VOLP. I think she loves me.
MOS.   Who? the lady, sir?
   She's jealous of you.
VOLP   Dost thou say so?   [*Knocking without*
MOS.   Hark,
   There's some already.

---

98 *count-book:* account-book.   100 *parcels:* goods.   107 *clarissimo:*
grandee (i.e., Corbaccio).   108 *crump you:* curl up.   *hog-louse:* wood-
louse.   120 *shroud:* disguise.

VOLP.   Look.
MOS.   It is the vulture:
  He has the quickest scent.
VOLP.   I'll to my place,
  Thou to thy posture.
MOS.   I am set.
VOLP.   But, Mosca,
  Play the artificer now, torture 'em rarely.

Enter VOLTORE

VOLT. How now, my Mosca?
MOS. [*writing*]   Turkey carpets, nine —
VOLT. Taking an inventory? that is well.   130
MOS. Two suits of bedding, tissue —
VOLT.   Where's the will?
  Let me read that the while.

Enter servants with CORBACCIO *in a chair*

CORB.   So, set me down,
  And get you home.
VOLT.   Is he come now, to trouble us?
MOS. Of cloth of gold, two more —
CORB.   Is it done, Mosca?
MOS. Of several velvets, eight —
VOLT.   I like his care.
CORB. Dost thou not hear?

Enter CORVINO

CORV.   Ha? is the hour come, Mosca?
VOLP. [*peeps from behind a traverse*] Aye, now they muster.
CORV.   What does the advocate here?
  Or this Corbaccio?
CORB.   What do these here?

Enter LADY POLITIC WOULD-BE

126 *to my place:* i.e., behind the curtain.   128 *artificer:* artist.
131 *tissue:* rich fabric.   137 (s.d.) *traverse:* curtain.

LADY P.   Mosca!
  Is his thread spun?
MOS.   Eight chests of linen —
VOLP.   O,
  My fine dame Would-be, too!
CORV.   Mosca, the will,   140
  That I may show it these, and rid 'em hence.
MOS. Six chests of diaper, four of damask — There.
                  [*Gives them the will carelessly over his shoulder*
CORB. Is that the will?
MOS.   Down-beds, and bolsters —
VOLP.   Rare!
  Be busy still. Now they begin to flutter:
  They never think of me. Look, see, see, see!
  How their swift eyes run over the long deed,
  Unto the name, and to the legacies,
  What is bequeath'd them there —
MOS.   Ten suits of hangings —
VOLP. Aye, i' their garters, Mosca. Now their hopes
  Are at the gasp.
VOLT.   Mosca the heir!
CORB.   What's that?   150
VOLP. My advocate is dumb; look to my merchant,
  He has heard of some strange storm, a ship is lost,
  He faints: my lady will swoon. Old glazen-eyes,
  He hath not reach'd his despair yet.
CORB.   All these
  Are out of hope, I am sure the man.   [*Takes the will*
CORV.   But, Mosca —
MOS. Two cabinets —
CORV.   Is this in earnest?
MOS.   One
  Of ebony. —

142 *diaper*: linen fabric.   *damask*: patterned woven silk.   143 *down-beds*: feather beds.   148 *suits of hangings*: sets of wall tapestry (Volpone plays on the other sense of 'hanging'; hanging yourself in your garters was a possible if rather comic way of committing suicide).   150 *at the gasp*: ready to die.

CORV.   Or do you but delude me?

MOS. The other, mother of pearl — I am very busy.
Good faith, it is a fortune thrown upon me —
Item, one salt of agate — not my seeking.   160

LADY P. Do you hear, sir?

MOS.   A perfum'd box — 'pray you forbear,
You see I am troubled — made of an onyx —

LADY P.   How!

MOS. To-morrow or next day I shall be at leisure
To talk with you all.

CORV.   Is this my large hope's issue?

LADY P. Sir, I must have a fairer answer.

MOS.   Madam!
Marry, and shall: 'pray you, fairly quit my house.
Nay, raise no tempest with your looks; but hark you:
Remember what your ladyship offered me
To put you in an heir; go to, think on 't.
And what you said e'en your best madams did   170
For maintenance, and why not you? Enough.
Go home, and use the poor Sir Pol, your knight, well,
For fear I tell some riddles: go, be melancholy.

VOLP. O, my fine devil!

CORV.   Mosca, 'pray you a word.

MOS. Lord! will not you take your dispatch hence yet?
                    [*Exit* LADY POLITIC WOULD-BE
Methinks of all, you should have been th' example.
Why should you stay here? with what thought, what
    promise?
Hear you, do not you know, I know you an ass?
And that you would most fain have been a wittol,
If fortune would have let you? that you are   180
A declar'd cuckold, on good terms? This pearl,
You'll say, was yours? right: this diamond?
I'll not deny 't, but thank you. Much here else?

160 *salt:* salt-cellar. 164 *issue:* outcome. 171 *maintenance:* to keep
themselves. 173 *tell some riddles:* tell some secrets. 179 *wittol:* a
husband who connives in his wife's infidelity.

It may be so. Why, think that these good works
May help to hide your bad: I'll not betray you,
Although you be but extraordinary,
And have it only in title, it sufficeth.

Go home, be melancholy too, or mad.   [*Exit* CORVINO

VOLP. Rare Mosca! how his villainy becomes him!

VOLT. [*aside*] Certain he doth delude all these for me.   190

CORB. Mosca the heir?

VOLP.   O, his four eyes have found it!

CORB. I am cozen'd, cheated, by a parasite slave;
    Harlot, th' hast gull'd me.

MOS.   Yes, sir. Stop your mouth,
    Or I shall draw the only tooth is left.
    Are not you he, that filthy covetous wretch
    With the three legs, that here, in hope of prey,
    Have, any time this three year, snuff'd about
    With your most grovelling nose; and would have hir'd
    Me to the poisoning of my patron, sir?
    Are not you he that have to-day, in court,   200
    Profess'd the disinheriting of your son?
    Perjur'd yourself? Go home, and die, and stink;
    If you but croak a syllable, all comes out:
    Away and call your porters! Go, go, stink.

                                   [*Exit* CORBACCIO

VOLP. Excellent varlet!

VOLT.   Now, my faithful Mosca,
    I find thy constancy . . .

MOS.   Sir?

VOLT.   Sincere.

MOS.   A table
    Of porphyry — I mar'l you'll be thus troublesome.

VOLT. Nay, leave off now, they are gone.

MOS.   Why? who are you?
    What? who did send for you? O cry you mercy,
    Reverend sir! good faith, I am griev'd for you,   210

193 *Harlot:* rogue (originally used of men). 204 *porters:* chairmen,
who carry Corvino about. 207 *mar'l:* marvel.

That any chance of mine should thus defeat
Your (I must needs say) most deserving travails:
But I protest, sir, it was cast upon me,
And I could almost wish to be without it,
But that the will of th' dead must be observ'd.
Marry, my joy is that you need it not,
You have a gift, sir (thank your education),
Will never let you want while there are men
And malice to breed causes. Would I had
But half the like for all my fortune, sir.   220
If I have any suits (as I do hope,
Things being so easy and direct, I shall not)
I will make bold with your obstreperous aid,
Conceive me for your fee, sir. In meantime,
You, that have so much law, I know ha' the conscience
Not to be covetous of what is mine.
Good sir, I thank you for my plate: 'twill help
To set up a young man. Good faith, you look
As you were costive; best go home and purge, sir.

                                   [*Exit* VOLTORE

VOLP. [*comes from behind curtain*] Bid him eat lettuce well: my
    witty mischief,   230
    Let me embrace thee. O, that I could now
    Transform thee to a Venus! Mosca, go
    Straight, take my habit of *clarissimo*,
    And walk the streets; be seen, torment 'em more:
    We must pursue, as well as plot. Who would
    Have lost this feast?
MOS.   I doubt it will lose them.
VOLP. O, my recovery shall recover all.
    That I could now but think on some disguise
    To meet 'em in, and ask 'em questions.
    How I would vex 'em still at every turn!   240
MOS. Sir, I can fit you.
VOLP.   Canst thou?

---

212 *travails:* labours. 229 *costive:* constipated. 230 *lettuce:* as a laxative.
233 *habit:* costume. 236 *lose them:* make them never come back.

MOS.   Yes, I know
　One o' the *commandadori*, sir, so like you;
　Him will I straight make drunk, and bring you his habit.
VOLP. A rare disguise, and answering thy brain!
　O, I will be a sharp disease unto 'em.
MOS. Sir, you must look for curses —
VOLP.   Till they burst;
　The Fox fares ever best when he is curs'd.   [*Exeunt*

Scene II

[*A hall in* SIR POLITIC'*s house*]
Enter PEREGRINE *disguised, and three* MERCHANTS

PER. Am I enough disguis'd?
1 MER.   I warrant you.
PER. All my ambition is to fright him only.
2 MER. If you could ship him away, 'twere excellent.
3 MER. To Zant or to Aleppo?
PER.   Yes, and ha' his
　Adventures put i' the Book of Voyages,
　And his gull'd story registered for truth.
　Well, gentlemen, when I am in a while,
　And that you think us warm in our discourse,
　Know your approaches.
1 MER.   Trust it to our care.   [*Exeunt* MERCHANTS

Enter WAITING-WOMAN

PER. Save you, fair lady. Is Sir Pol within?   10
WOM. I do not know, sir.
PER.   'Pray you, say unto him,
　Here is a merchant, upon earnest business,
　Desires to speak with him.
WOM.   I will see, sir.   [*Exit*

242 *so like you:* if it please you. 1 *I warrant you:* I guarantee you are.
4 *Zant:* Zacynthos, a Greek island. 5 *Book of Voyages:* collection
of travels (such as Hakluyt's). 9 *know your approaches:* know it is time
for you to approach.

PER.   'Pray you.
   I see the family is all female here.

Re-enter WOMAN

WOM. He says, sir, he had weighty affairs of state
   That now require him whole. Some other time
   You may possess him.
PER.   'Pray you, say again,
   If those require him whole, these will exact him
   Whereof I bring him tidings. [*Exit* WOMAN] What might be
   His grave affair of state now? how to make   20
   Bolognian sausages here in Venice, sparing
   One o' th' ingredients?

Re-enter WOMAN

WOM.   Sir, he says he knows
   By your word 'tidings' that you are no statesman,
   And therefore wills you stay.
PER.   Sweet, 'pray you return him
   I have not read so many proclamations,
   And studied them for words, as he has done,
   But — here he deigns to come.   [*Exit* WOMAN

Enter SIR POLITIC

POL.   Sir, I must crave
   Your courteous pardon. There hath chanc'd to-day
   Unkind disaster 'twixt my lady and me:
   And I was penning my apology,   30
   To give her satisfaction, as you came now.
PER. Sir, I am griev'd I bring you worse disaster;
   The gentleman you met at th' port to-day,
   That told you he was newly arriv'd —
POL.   Aye, was
   A fugitive punk?

16 *whole:* wholly.   17 *possess him:* have his attention.   18 *exact him:* completely absorb him.   21 *Bolognian:* from Bologna ('polonies').   23 *'tidings':* used instead of 'intelligence'.   35 *punk:* prostitute.

I

PER.   No, sir, a spy set on you:
And he has made relation to the Senate
That you profest to him to have a plot
To sell the state of Venice to the Turk.

POL. O me!

PER.   For which warrants are sign'd by this time,
To apprehend you, and to search your study   40
For papers —

POL.   Alas, sir I have none, but notes
Drawn out of play-books —

PER.   All the better, sir.

POL. And some essays. What shall I do?

PER.   Sir, best
Convey yourself into a sugar-chest,
Or, if you could lie round, a frail were rare,
And I could send you aboard.

POL.   Sir, I but talk'd so
For discourse sake, merely.   [They knock without

PER.   Hark, they are there.

POL. I am a wretch, a wretch.

PER.   What will you do, sir?
Ha' you ne'er a currant-butt to leap into?
They'll put you to the rack, you must be sudden.   50

POL. Sir, I have an ingine —

3 MER. [without]   Sir Politic Would-be?

2 MER. [without] Where is he?

POL.   That I have thought upon before time.

PER. What is it?

POL.   I shall ne'er endure the torture.
Marry, it is, sir, of a tortoise-shell,
Fitted for these extremities: pray you, sir, help me.
Here, I have a place, sir, to put back my legs;
Please you to lay it on, sir, [he lies down while PEREGRINE
    places the shell upon him] — with this cap

---

45 lie round: curl up. frail: rush basket, used for packing fruit.
49 currant-butt: barrel for currants (or currant-wine). 50 sudden: quick.
51 ingine: idea, device.

And my black gloves. I'll lie, sir, like a tortoise,
Till they are gone.

PER.   And call you this an ingine?

POL. Mine own device — good sir, bid my wife's women   60
To burn my papers.   [*Exit* PEREGRINE

The MERCHANTS *rush in*

1 MER.   Where's he hid?

3 MER.   We must
And will sure find him.

2 MER.   Which is his study?

Re-enter PEREGRINE

1 MER.   What
Are you, sir?

PER.   I am a merchant, that came here
To look upon this tortoise.

3 MER.   How?

1 MER.   St. Mark!
What beast is this?

PER.   It is a fish.

2 MER.   Come out here.

PER. Nay, you may strike him, sir, and tread upon him:
He'll bear a cart.

1 MER.   What, to run over him?

PER.   Yes.

3 MER. Let's jump upon him.

2 MER.   Can he not go?

PER.   He creeps, sir.

1 MER. Let's see him creep.

PER.   No, good sir, you will hurt him.

2 MER. Heart, I'll see him creep, or prick his guts.   70

3 MER. Come out here.

PER.   'Pray you, sir — [*aside to* SIR POLITIC
WOULD-BE] Creep a little.

1 MER.   Forth.

2 MER. Yet farther.

PER.   Good sir, creep. [*aside to* SIR POLITIC
    WOULD-BE]
2 MER.   We'll see his legs.
3 MER. Gods so, he has garters!
I MER.   Aye, and gloves.
                [*They pull off the shell and discover him*
2 MER.   Is this
    Your fearful tortoise?
PER.   Now, Sir Pol, we are even;
    For your next project I shall be prepar'd:
    I am sorry for the funeral of your notes, sir.
I MER. 'Twere a rare motion to be seen in Fleet-street!
2 MER. Aye, i' the term.
I MER.   Or Smithfield, in the fair.
3 MER. Methinks 'tis but a melancholy sight!
PER. Farewell, most politic tortoise.
                        [*Exeunt* PEREGRINE *and* MERCHANTS

            Re-enter WAITING-WOMAN

POL.   Where's my lady?   80
    Knows she of this?
WOM.   I know not, sir.
POL.   Enquire.
    O, I shall be the fable of all feasts,
    The freight of the *gazetti*; ship-boy's tale;
    And, which is worst, even talk for ordinaries.
WOM. My lady's come most melancholy home,
    And says, sir, she will straight to sea, for physic.
POL. And I to shun this place and clime for ever,
    Creeping with house on back, and think it well
    To shrink my poor head in my politic shell.   [*Exeunt*

77 *motion:* puppet-show.   78 *i' the term:* during the legal term,
when the law-courts are open.   80 *politic:* cunning, statesmanlike.
83 *freight of the gazetti:* subject for the newspapers. 84 *ordinaries:*
eating-houses.

Scene III

[*A room in* VOLPONE's *house*]
Enter VOLPONE *and* MOSCA. *The first in the habit of a com-*
mandadore: the other, of a clarissimo

VOLP. Am I then like him?
MOS.   O, sir, you are he:
  No man can sever you.
VOLP.   Good.
MOS.   But what am I?
VOLP. 'Fore heav'n, a brave *clarissimo*, thou becom'st it!
  Pity thou wert not born one.
MOS. [*aside*]   If I hold
  My made one, 'twill be well.
VOLP.   I'll go and see
  What news first at the court.   [*Exit*
MOS.   Do so. My Fox
  Is out of his hole and ere he shall re-enter
  I'll make him languish in his borrow'd case,
  Except he come to composition with me:
  Androgyno, Castrone, Nano!

Enter ANDROGYNO, NANO, *and* CASTRONE

ALL.   Here.   10
MOS. Go recreate yourselves abroad; go sport: [*Exeunt*
  So, now I have the keys, and am possessed.
  Since he will needs be dead afore his time,
  I'll bury him, or gain by him. I am his heir:
  And so will keep me, till he share at least.
  To cozen him of all were but a cheat
  Well plac'd; no man would construe it a sin:
  Let his sport pay for 't, this is call'd the Fox-trap. [*Exit*

2 *sever you:* distinguish between you. 8 *case:* skin. 9 *composition:*
terms, agreement. 16 *cozen:* do him out of.

Scene IV

[*A street*]

Enter CORBACCIO *and* CORVINO

CORB. They say the court is set.

CORV.   We must maintain
Our first tale good, for both our reputations.

CORB. Why? mine's no tale: my son would there have kill'd me.

CORV. That's true, I had forgot: [*aside*] mine is, I'm sure.
But for your will, sir.

CORB.   I'll come upon him
For that hereafter, now his patron's dead.

Enter VOLPONE *disguised*

VOLP. Signior Corvino! and Corbaccio! sir,
Much joy unto you.

CORV.   Of what?

VOLP.   The sudden good
Dropp'd down upon you —

CORB.   Where?

VOLP.   And none knows how,
From old Volpone, sir.

CORB.   Out, arrant knave.   10

VOLP. Let not your too much wealth sir, make you furious.

CORB. Away, thou varlet.

VOLP.   Why, sir?

CORB.   Dost thou mock me?

VOLP. You mock the world, sir; did you not change wills?

CORB. Out, harlot.

VOLP.   O! belike you are the man,
Signior Corvino? 'faith, you carry it well;
You grow not mad withal: I love your spirit.
You are not over-leaven'd with your fortune.
You should ha' some would swell now, like a wine-fat
With such an autumn — Did he gi' you all, sir?

1 *set:* in session.   17 *over-leaven'd:* too much puffed-up.   18 *wine-fat:* wine-vat.

CORV. Avoid, you rascal.

VOLP.   Troth, your wife has shown   20
   Herself a very woman: but you are well,
   You need not care, you have a good estate,
   To bear it out, sir, better by this chance —
   Except Corbaccio have a share?

CORB.   Hence, varlet.

VOLP. You will not be a'known, sir: why, 'tis wise.
   Thus do all gamesters, at all games, dissemble.
   No man will seem to win.

                    [*Exeunt* CORVINO *and* CORBACCIO
                        Here comes my vulture,
   Heaving his beak up i' the air, and snuffing.

                    Enter VOLTORE

VOLT. Outstript thus, by a parasite? a slave,
   Would run on errands, and make legs for crumbs?   30
   Well, what I'll do —

VOLP.   The court stays for your worship.
   I e'en rejoice, sir, at your worship's happiness,
   And that it fell into so learned hands
   That understand the fingering —

VOLT.   What do you mean?

VOLP. I mean to be a suitor to your worship
   For the small tenement, out of reparations,
   That at the end of your long row of houses
   By the Piscaria: it was, in Volpone's time,
   Your predecessor, ere he grew diseas'd,
   A handsome, pretty, custom'd bawdy-house   40
   As any was in Venice (none disprais'd),
   But fell with him; his body and that house
   Decay'd together.

VOLT.   Come, sir, leave your prating.

20 *avoid:* get out of the way.   21 *very:* true.   23 *bear it out:* carry
it off.   24 *except:* unless.   25 *a'known:* acknowledged (as the heir).
30 *make legs:* bow, cringe.   34 *fingering:* the way to do things.
36 *reparations:* repairs.   38 *Piscaria:* the fish-market.   40 *custom'd:*
well frequented, popular.

VOLP. Why, if your worship give me but your hand
  That I may ha' the refusal, I have done.
  'Tis a mere toy to you, sir; candle-rents:
  As your learn'd worship knows —
VOLT.   What do I know?
VOLP. Marry, no end of your wealth, sir, God decrease it!
VOLT. Mistaking knave! what, mock'st thou my misfortune?
                                                      [*Exit*

VOLP. His blessing on your heart, sir, would 'twere more.   50
  Now to my first again at the next corner.   [*Exit*

Enter CORBACCIO *and* CORVINO. MOSCA *passes over the stage
                      before them*

CORB. See, in our habit! see the impudent varlet!
CORV. That I could shoot mine eyes at him, like gun-stones.

Enter VOLPONE

VOLP. But is this true, sir, of the parasite?
CORB. Again t' afflict us? monster!
VOLP.   In good faith, sir,
  I am heartily griev'd a beard of your grave length
  Should be so over-reach'd. I never brook'd
  That parasite's hair, methought his nose should cozen:
  There still was somewhat in his look did promise
  The bane of a *clarissimo*.
CORB.   Knave —
VOLP.   Methinks   60
  Yet you that are so traded i' the world,
  A witty merchant, the fine bird, Corvino,
  That have such moral emblems on your name,
  Should not have sung your shame, and dropp'd your cheese,
  To let the Fox laugh at your emptiness.
CORV. Sirrah, you think the privilege of the place,

46 *candle-rents:* a low rent from valueless property.   48 *decrease:* (a
deliberate mistake by Volpone for 'increase').   53 *gun-stones:* cannon-
balls.   57 *brook'd:* endured.   63 *moral emblems:* (alluding to the fables
of the Fox and the Crow).

And your red saucy cap, that seems to me
Nail'd to your jolt-head with those two *cecchines*,
Can warrant your abuses; come you hither:
You shall perceive, sir, I dare beat you. Approach.   70
VOLP. No haste, sir, I do know your valour well,
Since you durst publish what you are, sir.
CORV.   Tarry,
I'd speak with you.
VOLP.   Sir, sir, another time —
CORV. Nay, now.
VOLP.   O God, sir! I were a wise man
Would stand the fury of a distracted cuckold.

MOSCA *walks by*

CORB. What! come again?
VOLP.   Upon 'em, Mosca; save me.
CORB. The air's infected where he breathes.
CORV.   Let's fly him. [*Exeunt* CORVINO *and* CORBACCIO
VOLP. Excellent basilisk! turn upon the vulture.

Enter VOLTORE

VOLT. Well, flesh-fly, it is summer with you now;
Your winter will come on.
MOS.   Good advocate,   80
'Pray thee, not rail, nor threaten out of place thus;
Thou'lt make a solecism, as madam says.
Get you a biggin more: your brain breaks loose.   [*Exit*
VOLT. Well, sir.
VOLP.   Would you ha' me beat the insolent slave?
Throw dirt upon his first good clothes?
VOLT.   This same
Is doubtless some familiar!
VOLP.   Sir, the court

67–8 *red saucy cap . . . cecchines:* (the commandadore wore a red cap
with two gilt buttons in front).   68 *jolt-head:* blockhead.   69 *warrant
your abuses:* let you insult people with impunity.   78 *basilisk:* mythical
monster whose look turned people to stone.   79 *flesh-fly:* bluebottle.
83 *biggin:* a lawyer's cap.

In troth stays for you. I am mad, a mule
That never read Justinian should get up
And ride an advocate. Had you no quirk
To avoid gullage, sir, by such a creature?   90
I hope you do but jest; he has not done 't:
This's but confederacy to blind the rest.
You are the heir?

VOLT.   A strange, officious,
Troublesome knave! thou dost torment me.

VOLP.   I know —
It cannot be, sir, that you should be cozen'd;
'Tis not within the wit of man to do it:
You are so wise, so prudent, and 'tis fit
That wealth and wisdom still should go together.   [*Exeunt*

Scene V

[*The Senate House*]

Enter AVOCATORI, NOTARIO, COMMANDADORI, BONARIO,
CELIA, CORBACCIO, CORVINO, *etc.*

1 AVOC. Are all the parties here?
NOT.   All but the advocate.
2 AVOC. And here he comes.

Enter VOLTORE *and* VOLPONE

1 AVOC.   Then bring 'em forth to sentence.
VOLT. O my most honour'd fathers, let your mercy
Once win upon your justice, to forgive —
I am distracted —
VOLP. [*aside*]   What will he do now?
VOLT.   O,
I know not which t' address myself to first,
Whether your fatherhoods, or these innocents —

86 *familiar:* familiar spirit, demon. 89 *quirk:* trick. 90 *gullage:* being
made a fool of. 92 *confederacy:* plot.

CORV. [*aside*] Will he betray himself?
VOLT.   Whom equally
   I have abus'd, out of most covetous ends —
CORV. The man is mad!
CORB.   What's that?
CORV.   He is possess'd.   10
VOLT. For which, now struck in conscience, here I prostrate
   Myself at your offended feet, for pardon.
1, 2 AVOC. Arise.
CEL.   O heav'n, how just thou art!
VOLP. [*aside*]   I am caught
   I' mine own noose —
CORV. [*to* CORBACCIO] Be constant, sir, nought now
   Can help but impudence.
1 AVOC.   Speak forward.
COM.   Silence.
VOLT. It is not passion in me, reverend fathers,
   But only conscience, conscience, my good sires,
   That makes me now tell truth. That parasite,
   That knave, hath been the instrument of all.
2 AVOC. Where is that knave? fetch him.
VOLP.   I go.   [*Exit*
CORV.   Grave fathers,   20
   This man's distracted; he confess'd it now:
   For, hoping to be old Volpone's heir,
   Who now is dead —
3 AVOC.   How?
2 AVOC.   Is Volpone dead?
CORV. Dead since, grave fathers —
BON.   O, sure vengeance!
1 AVOC.   Stay;
   Then he was no deceiver?
VOLT.   O no, none:
   The parasite, grave fathers.
CORV.   He does speak
   Out of mere envy 'cause the servant's made

         10 *possess'd:* i.e. by a devil.

The thing he gap'd for; please your fatherhoods,
This is the truth: though I'll not justify
The other, but he may be some-deal faulty.   30

VOLT. Aye, to your hopes, as well as mine, Corvino:
But I'll use modesty. Pleaseth your wisdoms
To view these certain notes, and but confer them;
As I hope favour, they shall speak clear truth.

CORV. The devil has entered him!

BON.   Or bides in you.

4 AVOC. We have done ill, by a public officer
To send for him, if he be heir.

2 AVOC.   For whom?

4 AVOC. Him that they call the parasite.

3 AVOC.   'Tis true;
He is a man of great estate, now left.

4 AVOC. Go you and learn his name; and say the court   40
Entreats his presence here, but to the clearing
Of some few doubts.   [Exit NOTARIO

2 AVOC.   This same's a labyrinth!

1 AVOC. Stand you unto your first report?

CORV.   My state,
My life, my fame —

BON.   Where is 't?

CORV.   Are at the stake.

1 AVOC. Is yours so too?

CORB.   The advocate's a knave,
And has a forked tongue —

2 AVOC.   Speak to the point.

CORB. So is the parasite too.

1 AVOC.   This is confusion.

VOLT. I do beseech your fatherhoods, read but those —
                              [Gives them papers

CORV. And credit nothing the false spirit hath writ:
It cannot be but he is possess'd, grave fathers.   50

---

28 *gap'd for:* longed for.   30 *some-deal:* somewhat.   32 *modesty:* moderation.   33 *confer them:* compare them.

Scene VI

[The street]
Enter VOLPONE

VOLP. To make a snare for mine own neck! and run
   My head into it wilfully! with laughter!
   When I had newly scap'd, was free and clear!
   Out of mere wantonness! O, the dull devil
   Was in this brain of mine when I devis'd it;
   And Mosca gave it second: he must now
   Help to sear up this vein, or we bleed dead.

Enter NANO, ANDROGYNO, *and* CASTRONE

   How now! who let you loose? whither go you now?
   What? to buy gingerbread? or to drown kitlings?
NAN. Sir, Master Mosca call'd us out of doors,   10
   And bid us all go play, and took the keys.
AND.   Yes.
VOLP. Did Master Mosca take the keys? why, so!
   I am farther in. These are my fine conceits!
   I must be merry with a mischief to me!
   What a vile wretch was I, that could not bear
   My fortune soberly I must ha' my crotchets
   And my conundrums! well, go you and seek him:
   His meaning may be truer than my fear.
   Bid him he straight come to me to the court;
   Thither will I, and, if 't be possible.   20
   Unscrew my advocate, upon new hopes:
   When I provok'd him, then I lost myself.   *[Exeunt*

6 *gave it second:* supported it. 7 *sear up:* close up by cautery.
16 *crotchets:* fancies, whims.

Scene VII

[*The Senate House*]

AVOCATORI, BONARIO, CELIA, CORBACCIO, CORVINO,
COMMANDADORI, SAFFI, *etc., as before*

1 AVOC. These things can ne'er be reconcil'd. He here
    Professeth that the gentleman was wrong'd,
    And that the gentlewoman was brought thither,
    Forc'd by her husband, and there left.

VOLT.   Most true.

CEL. How ready is heav'n to those that pray!

1 AVOC.   But that
    Volpone would have ravish'd her, he holds
    Utterly false knowing his impotence.

CORV. Grave fathers, he is possess'd; again, I say,
    Possess'd: nay, if there be possession and
    Obsession, he has both.

3 AVOC.   Here comes our officer.   10

Enter VOLPONE

VOLP. The parasite will straight be here, grave fathers.

4 AVOC. You might invent some other name, sir varlet.

3 AVOC. Did not the notary meet him?

VOLP.   Not that I know.

4 AVOC. His coming will clear all.

2 AVOC.   Yet it is misty.

VOLT. May't please your fatherhoods —

VOLP. [*whispers to* VOLTORE]   Sir, the parasite
    Will'd me to tell you that his master lives;
    That you are still the man; your hopes the same;
    And this was only a jest —

VOLT.   How?

VOLP.   Sir, to try
    If you were firm, and how you stood affected.

VOLT. Art' sure he lives?

VOLP.   Do I live, sir?

VOLT.   O, me!   20
  I was too violent.
VOLP.   Sir, you may redeem it:
  They said you were possess'd; fall down, and seem so:
  I'll help to make it good. [VOLTORE *falls*] God bless the
    man!
  — Stop your wind hard, and swell — see, see, see, see!
  He vomits crooked pins! his eyes are set
  Like a dead hare's hung in a poulter's shop!
  His mouth's running away! do you see, signior?
  Now 'tis in his belly.
CORV. [*aside*]   Aye, the devil!
VOLP. Now in his throat.
CORV.   Aye, I perceive it plain.
VOLP. 'Twill out, 'twill out; stand clear. See where it flies,   30
  In shape of a blue toad, with a bat's wings!
  Do not you see it, sir?
CORB.   What? I think I do.
CORV. 'Tis too manifest.
VOLP.   Look! he comes t' himself!
VOLT. Where am I?
VOLP.   Take good heart, the worst is past, sir.
  You are dispossess'd.
I AVOC.   What accident is this?
2 AVOC. Sudden, and full of wonder.
3 AVOC.   If he were
  Possess'd, as it appears, all this is nothing.
CORV. He has been often subject to these fits.
I AVOC. Show him that writing; do you know it, sir?
VOLP. [*aside to* VOLTORE] Deny it, sir, forswear it, know   40
  it not.
VOLT. Yes, I do know it well, it is my hand:
  But all that it contains is false.
BON.   O practice!
2 AVOC. What maze is this!
I AVOC.   Is he not guilty, then,

42 *practice:* perjury, deceit.

Whom you there name the parasite?

VOLT.   Grave fathers,
No more than his good patron, old Volpone.

4 AVOC. Why, he is dead.

VOLT.   O no, my honour'd fathers.
He lives —

1 AVOC.   How! lives?

VOLT.   Lives.

2 AVOC.   This is subtler yet!

3 AVOC. You said he was dead.

VOLT.   Never.

3 AVOC.   You said so.

CORV.   I heard so.

4 AVOC. Here comes the gentleman, make him way.

Enter MOSCA

3 AVOC.   A stool.

4 AVOC. [*aside*] A proper man! and, were Volpone dead,   50
A fit match for my daughter.

3 AVOC.   Give him way.

VOLP. [*aside to* MOSCA] Mosca, I was a'most lost; the
    advocate,
    Had betray'd all; but now it is recover'd:
    All's o' the hinge again — say I am living.

MOS. What busy knave is this! Most reverend fathers,
    I sooner had attended your grave pleasures
    But that my order for the funeral
    Of my dear patron did require me —

VOLP. [*aside*]   Mosca!

MOS. Whom I intend to bury like a gentleman.

VOLP. [*aside*] Aye, quick, and cozen me of all

2 AVOC.   Still stranger!   60
    More intricate!

1 AVOC.   And come about again?

4 AVOC. [*aside*] It is a match, my daughter is bestow'd.

54 *o' the hinge:* in working order.   55 *busy:* officious.   60 *quick:* alive.

MOS. [*aside to* VOLPONE] Will you gi' me half?

VOLP. [*aside*]   First, I'll be hang'd.

MOS. [*aside*]   I know.
   Your voice is good, cry not so loud.

I AVOC.   Demand
   The advocate. Sir, did not you affirm
   Volpone was alive?

VOLP.   Yes, and he is;
   This gent'man told me so. — [*To* MOSCA] Thou shalt have
     half.

MOS. Whose drunkard is this same? speak, some that know
     him:
   I never saw his face. — [*To* VOLPONE] I cannot now
   Afford it you so cheap.

VOLP. [*aside*]   No?

I AVOC.   What say you?   70

VOLT. The officer told me.

VOLP.   I did, grave fathers,
   And will maintain he lives with mine own life.
   And that this creature told me. [*aside*] I was born
   With all good stars my enemies.

MOS.   Most grave fathers,
   If such an insolence as this must pass
   Upon me, I am silent: 'twas not this
   For which you sent, I hope.

2 AVOC.   Take him away.

VOLP. Mosca!

3 AVOC.   Let him be whipp'd.

VOLP. [*to* MOSCA]   Wilt thou betray me?
   Cozen me?

3 AVOC. And taught to bear himself
   Toward a person of his rank.

4 AVOC.   Away.   80
                [*The officers seize* VOLPONE

MOS. I humbly thank your fatherhoods.

VOLP. [*aside*]   Soft, soft: whipp'd?
   And lose all that I have? If I confess,

K

It cannot be much more.

4 AVOC. [*to* MOSCA]   Sir, are you married?

VOLP. [*aside*] They'll be allied, anon; I must be resolute:
The Fox shall here uncase.   [*He puts off his disguise*

MOS.   Patron!

VOLP.   Nay, now
My ruins shall not come alone; your match
I'll hinder sure: my substance shall not glue you,
Nor screw you into a family.

MOS.   Why, patron!

VOLP. I am Volpone, and this is my knave;

                                        [*pointing to* MOSCA
This [*to* VOLTORE], his own knave; this [*to* CORBACCIO]
    avarice's fool;   90
This [*to* CORVINO], a chimera of wittol, fool, and knave;
And, reverend fathers, since we all can hope
Nought but a sentence, let's not now despair it.
You hear me brief.

CORV.   May it please your fatherhoods —

COM.   Silence.

1 AVOC. The knot is now undone by miracle!

2 AVOC. Nothing can be more clear.

3 AVOC.   Or can more prove
These innocent.

1 AVOC.   Give 'em their liberty.

BON. Heaven could not long let such gross crimes be hid.

2 AVOC. If this be held the highway to get riches,
May I be poor.

3 AVOC.   This 's not the gain, but torment.   100

1 AVOC. These possess wealth as sick men possess fevers,
Which trulier may be said to possess them.

2 AVOC. Disrobe that parasite.

CORV., MOS.   Most honour'd fathers —

1 AVOC. Can you plead ought to stay the course of justice?
If you can, speak.

85 *uncase:* unmask himself. 87 *substance:* property. 91 *chimera:* the
mythical chimera was a mixture of lion, goat, and snake.

CORV., VOLT.   We beg favour.
CEL.   And mercy.
1 AVOC. You hurt your innocence, suing for the guilty.
   Stand forth; and first the parasite. You appear
   T' have been the chiefest minister, if not plotter,
   In all these lewd impostures; and now, lastly,
   Have with your impudence abus'd the court,   110
   And habit of a gentleman of Venice,
   Being a fellow of no birth or blood:
   For which, our sentence is, first thou be whipp'd;
   Then live perpetual prisoner in our galleys.
VOLP. I thank you for him.
MOS.   Bane to thy wolvish nature!
1 AVOC. Deliver him to the *Saffi*.   [MOSCA *is carried out*
                Thou, Volpone,
   By blood and rank a gentleman, canst not fall
   Under like censure; but our judgement on thee
   Is that thy substance all be straight confiscate
   To the hospital of the *Incurabili*:   120
   And since the most was gotten by imposture,
   By feigning lame, gout, palsy, and such diseases,
   Thou art to lie in prison, cramp'd with irons,
   Till thou be'st sick and lame indeed. Remove him.
                [*He is taken from the Bar*
VOLP. This is call'd mortifying of a Fox.
1 AVOC. Thou, Voltore, to take away the scandal
   Thou hast giv'n all worthy men of thy profession,
   Art banish'd from their fellowship, and our state.
   Corbaccio! Bring him near. We here possess
   Thy son of all thy state, and confine thee   130
   To the monastery of San Spirito:
   Where, since thou knew'st not how to live well here,
   Thou shalt be learn'd to die well.
CORB.   Ha! what said he?
COM. You shall know anon, sir.
1 AVOC.   Thou, Corvino, shalt

        129 *possess:* give possession to.

Be straight embark'd from thine own house, and row'd
Round about Venice through the Grand Canal,
Wearing a cap with fair long ass's ears,
Instead of horns: and so to mount, a paper
Pinn'd to thy breast, to the *berlina* —

CORV.   Yes,
And have mine eyes beat out with stinking fish,   140
Bruis'd fruit, and rotten eggs — 'Tis well. I am glad
I shall not see my shame yet.

1 AVOC.   And to expiate
Thy wrongs done to thy wife, thou **art to** send her
Home to her father, with her dowry **trebled:**
And these are all your judgements.

ALL.   Honour'd fathers.

1 AVOC. Which may not be revok'd. Now you begin,
When crimes are done and past, and to be punish'd,
To think what your crimes are. Away with them!
Let all that see these vices thus rewarded
Take heart, and love to study 'em. Mischiefs feed   150
Like beasts, till they be fat, and then they bleed.   [*Exeunt*

VOLPONE *comes forward*

The seasoning of a play is the applause.
Now, though the Fox be punish'd by the laws,
He yet doth hope there is no suffering due
For any fact which he hath done 'gainst you;
If there be, censure him: here he doubtful stands.
If not, fare jovially, and clap your hands.

[*Exit*

139 *berlina:* the pillory.

THE END

Notes

PROLOGUE

ll. 11–12. Jonson was notoriously a slow worker, and his enemies frequently made fun of the fact.

ll. 16–17. Elizabethan plays were frequently written in collaboration. **Coadjutors** were authors of equal standing (like Beaumont and Fletcher) who collaborated by each writing a different part of the play. A **novice** was a beginner writing under the supervision of a more experienced author; a **journeyman** was an inferior writer brought in to write a particular part of the play; a **tutor** means a writer who corrected or improved a play after it was written.

ll. 20–1. A regular feature of City banquets was the production of a huge custard, into which the Fool jumped, but Jonson may only be thinking of the sort of slap-stick with custard-pies which still goes on in pantomimes and circuses.

l. 26. Beth'lem was the madhouse in London, best known as Bedlam, but properly called the Hospital of St. Mary Bethlehem. Jonson is saying that some plays have so much violent and extravagant 'business' that the only people who could enjoy or support them would be the inhabitants of Bedlam.

l. 31. The **laws of time, place, persons** are the famous 'Unities', drawn by neo-classical critics from Aristotle's *Poetics*. According to these 'rules' the action of a play should take place in one spot, the time taken by the action should not exceed twenty-four hours, and no characters and incidents should be introduced which were not strictly relevant to the plot. Jonson did not regard these rules as binding, but in *Volpone* all the action does take place in one city, everything could happen on the same day, and the only scenes which might be accused of irrelevance are those between Peregrine and Sir Politic Would-be.

ACT I

SCENE I

Jonson, in accordance with Neo-classical practice, does not give
any indication of place, and marks a new scene with the entry of
each character to the stage. In this edition a new scene is indicated
only where the location must be assumed to have changed.

l. 5. The Sun enters the sign of Aries in the Spring.

ll. 9–11. An allusion to the Creation.

ll. 42–3. The Dutch were famous for eating a lot of butter, and
were generally regarded as drunkards and gluttons.

ll. 90ff. In writing the curious Interlude which Nano, Androgyno
and Castrone perform for Volpone's entertainment, Jonson
used the halting metre (the 'false pace') of the old morality
plays, but he drew his material mainly from a dialogue
(*Gallus*, or the Cock) by Lucian (*c.* A.D. 115–*c.* A.D. 200).
This dialogue begins with Micyllus the cobbler cursing
his cock for having woken him up from a beautiful dream,
and being much surprised when the cock answers him back.
The cock explains that he contains the soul of the philosopher and mathematician Pythagoras (born about 520
B.C.). (Pythagoras maintained the doctrine of metempsy-
chosis or transmigration of souls, and according to some
accounts claimed to be able to remember his own previous
incarnations.) The soul was first incarnated as Aethalides,
one of the Argonauts; thence it passed to Euphorbus, a
Trojan killed at the siege of Troy by Menelaus ('the
cuckold of Sparta'); after this it went to Hermotimus and
then to Pyrrhus, a fisherman of Delos. After having been the
soul of Pythagoras ('the sophist of Greece') it went first to
Aspasia, the mistress of Pericles, and so to Crates the Cynic
philosopher, who lived in the fourth century B.C.; after
this it had various other adventures before ending up as
Micyllus' cock. In the interlude Jonson traces its descent
further into a Carthusian monk (where it learnt to eat fish —
Pythagoras was a vegetarian), a lawyer, a mule (where it
learnt to eat beans, which Pythagoras forbad to his followers), a Puritan, and so to Androgyno.

ll. 115–16. A great deal of Pythagoras' teaching was concerned

with the theory of numbers and their symbolism. The figure
1 symbolizes the underlying unity of creation; 2 among
other things symbolizes duality and contrariety; 3 is the
number of the three dimensions of solid shapes; 4 is the
number of the four elements — earth, air, fire and water —
of which everything is made, and which are constantly
changing one into another. Pythagoras swore by the Tetrad
('By Quater'): the Tetrad is a magical symbol of this
appearance:

$$
\begin{array}{cccc}
 & & \bullet & \\
 & \bullet & & \bullet \\
 \bullet & & \bullet & \\
\bullet & \bullet & \bullet & \bullet
\end{array}
$$

As will be seen, each side of this figure is of 4 units, and it
produces the sequence 1, 2, 3, 4, from whichever point one
starts; it also shows that the sum of $1+2+3+4$ is 10, the
perfect number.

l. 117. Some of his followers believed that Pythagoras was a
re-incarnation of Apollo, and that his limbs were of gold.

ll. 184–6. An allusion to the fable of the Fox and the Crow.

l. 373 Gold was much esteemed in the Middle Ages as a thera-
peutic agent, and was often included in medicines in the
form of gold-leaf or gold-dust.

l. 456. **Aeson,** father of Jason, was restored to youth by
Medea (who boiled him in a cauldron with magic herbs).

l. 476. A carat is 150th part of an ounce (troy).

ACT II

SCENE I

l. 14. Elizabethan travellers had to have a licence from the Privy
Council to travel abroad.

ll. 34ff. Some of the marvels which Peregrine relates actually
occurred: one of the lionesses in the Tower of London produced a cub in 1604 and another in 1605; at the end of 1604
it was reported that strange lights and noises had been

heard in the hills near Berwick; in October 1604 the astro-
nomer Kepler observed a *nova* or new star of exceptional
brightness. In 1600 a whale did come up the Thames nearly
as far as London; Peregrine suggests that this had something to do with the war in the Netherlands ('the Stode
fleet' is the Dutch fleet at Stade, on the mouth of the Elbe);
Sir Politic thinks it must have been a device of Spinola, the
Spanish Commander-in-Chief in the Netherlands, or of the
Spanish Archduke Albert of the Netherlands.

ll. 53ff. **Stone, the fool,** was a real person, mentioned by the
gossip-writers of the day, but little is known about him.

ll. 81–3. In Jacobean times meat was often served cut up into
curious shapes, and Sir Politic suggests that messages were
given to Stone in this way.

l. 90. The **Mamuluchi** or Mamelukes had nothing to do with
China, but were, in fact, Egyptian soldiers in the service of
the Sultan of Turkey.

l. 144. **Scoto of Mantua** was a real person, an Italian actor and
juggler, who visited England and performed before Queen
Elizabeth.

l. 158. The **Procuratia**, in the Piazza di San Marco, has a portico
or arcade in front of it.

ll. 167ff. Nothing is known of an **Alessandro Buttone,** but
Tabarin was a real 'zany' in a troop of Italian actors.
Cardinal Bembo (1470–1547) was a very famous scholar
and writer.

ll. 238–9. Volpone calls Nano **Zan Fritada,** which means 'John
Pancake' in Italian; there was, however, a real 'zany' by that
name.

ll. 242ff. **Hugh Broughton** (1549–1612) was a well-known
Puritan theologian. **Hippocrates** (fifth century B.C.) and
Galen (2nd century A.D.) were regarded as the founders of
all medical theory. **Lully** (1235–1315), a Catalan, was a
mystic, poet, scholar and philosopher, but is here referred
to as a magician. **Danish Gonswart** may be Jonson's
invention, or may be a German monk called Schwartz, who
is alleged to have invented fire-arms. **Paracelsus** (1493–
1541) was a chemist and doctor, but was also, like Lully,
regarded as a magician; he was famous for his sword, in the
pommel of which he was supposed to carry his medicines.

l. 302. **Cardinal Fernese** became Pope in 1534 (as Paul III);

Cardinal Montalto became Pope in 1585 (as Sixtus V). Cosimo de' Medici was created **Great Duke of Tuscany** in 1569.

ll. 373ff. Corvino treats Volpone and Celia as if they had been acting a play (Volpone is actually standing on a stage, of course, and Celia looking out of a window above him). **Flaminio Scala** was an actual actor in the Commedia dell' Arte at the time of *Volpone*; **Fransciscina** is the type-name of the servant in this type of drama, and **Pantalone** ('Pantaloon') is the type-name of the jealous old man. In II. iii. 21 Corvino addresses Celia as 'Lady Vanity' — a name from another kind of drama, the morality play.

SCENE III

ll. 23–4. If Corvino proclaims that Celia has been unfaithful to him, he will be able to get rid of her without having to return her dowry to her father.

ACT III

SCENE II

ll. 107ff. The poet Volpone refers to is Sophocles: Lady Would-be then proceeds to show off her culture by running through the names of the most famous modern Italian writers. **Guarini** (1537–1612) was best known in England for his pastoral drama *Pastor Fido*; **Aretino** (1492–1556) was most famous for a set of sixteen obscene sonnets written to accompany pictures by Giulio Romano; **Cieco di Hadria** (literally 'the blind man of Adria') was Luigi Groto (1541–1585), a less well-known, though very prolific writer.

ll. 193–5. **Draw** and **encounter** are terms used in the popular card-game **primero**, but Volpone also quibbles on the senses of 'encounter' = (a) a duel (for which one draws one's sword), and (b) a lovers' meeting.

ll. 196ff. The staging of the following scene is rather complicated. Volpone is in his bed, round which curtains can be drawn, on one side of the stage, which would have, in the Jacobean theatre, two doors at the back. Bonario is brought in by

Mosca through one door, and is placed behind a screen on the opposite side of the stage from Volpone. Corvino and Celia come in at the other door, go to the back of that stage at 'Hark hither' (l. 209), come forward at l. 219, and are brought by Mosca up to Volpone's bed at l. 269.

ll. 360–1 **Henry of Valois,** afterwards Henry III of France, was entertained by the Doge and Senators of Venice in 1574. **Antinous** was a favourite of the Roman Emperor Hadrian.

l. 390. The **brave Egyptian queen** is of course Cleopatra, and the reference is to the banquet where she swallowed a pearl dissolved in vinegar. This story is told by Pliny in his *Natural History* and in the same passage he recounts having seen **Lollia Paulina,** wife of the Emperor Caligula, wearing jewels worth forty million sesterces (over one million pounds) which she had inherited from her grandfather, who had gained them, in part as spoils, in part as bribes, from Eastern kings.

ACT IV

SCENE I

l. 26. **Niccolo Machiavelli** (1459–1527) was chiefly known in England as the author of *The Prince*, and was regarded as completely unscrupulous and amoral; **Jean Bodin** (1530–1596), the French political philosopher, was an advocate of religious toleration, and was sometimes called an atheist.

ll. 27–9. The use of forks for eating with was an Italian custom still little followed in England at the time of *Volpone*; Venetian glass was (and is) famous. **Metal** is the technical name for molten glass when it is ready for blowing.

l. 40. **Cardinal Contarini** wrote an account of Venice which appeared in English in 1599.

ll. 74–5. The **Great Council** of Venice consisted of all gentlemen over the age of twenty-five (about one thousand in number); the Ten were ten members of the Senate especially concerned with offences against the State; there were actually three 'Colleges' each of forty magistrates, who tried civil and criminal cases. Sir Politic, as perhaps we might expect, does not seem very clear about the Venetian constitution.

ll. 148–9. 'Fast and loose' was a sort of game in which the player had to fasten a belt to the table with a dagger or pin; the belt was folded in such a way that it looked as if it was fast when it was not. Gipsies were expert at this, and it became a byword for deceit and trickery.

l. 195. **Sporus** was a favourite of the Emperor Nero.

l. 198. **Whitefriars** in London was originally a 'liberty' or sanctuary, and as such was frequented by criminals and prostitutes.

SCENE II

l. 22. **Hercules** visited France in carrying out one of his labours and was regarded as the founder of the Celtic race, and in this capacity as the father of eloquence.

l. 152. Jacobean children learned their ABC from a 'hornbook', which looked rather like a table-tennis bat with the alphabet and the Lord's Prayer pasted on the flat part, and was held in the hand. The letters were covered by a piece of transparent horn to protect them. Corvino is playing on the favourite joke about the horns that were supposed to spring from the forehead of a man whose wife had been unfaithful to him.

ACT V

SCENE I

ll. 119–21. The **strange poetical girdle** is the *cestus* of Venus, embroidered with devices to stir love, which Homer describes in Bk. IV of the *Iliad*. **Acrisius** was the father of Danae; he shut her up in a tower, but Jupiter visited her in the form of a shower of gold.

ll. 185–7. Corvino is not really a cuckold, though he has proclaimed himself one; he therefore has the title 'extraordinary', like a Suffragan Bishop, who has the title of Bishop though he does not have a See.

Critical Extracts

As for *Johnson*, to whose Character I am now arriv'd, if we look upon him while he was himself, (for his last plays were but his dotages) I think him the most learned and judicious Writer which any Theater ever had. He was a most severe Judge of himself as well as others. One cannot say he wanted wit, but rather that he was frugal of it. In his works you will find little to retrench or alter. Wit and Language, and Humour also in some measure we had before him; but something of Art was wanting to the *Drama* till he came. He manag'd his strength to more advantage than any who preceded him. You seldom find him making Love in any of his Scenes, or endeavouring to move the Passions; his genius was too sullen and saturnine to do it gracefully, especially when he knew he came after those who had performed both to such an height. Humour was his proper Sphere, and in that he delighted most to represent Mechanick people. He was deeply conversant in the Ancients, both Greek and Latin, and he borrow'd boldly from them. . . . But he has done his Robberies so openly, that one may see he fears not to be taxed by any Law. He invades Authours like a Monarch, and what would be theft in other Poets, is only victory in him . . . If I would compare him with *Shakespeare*, I must acknowledge him the more correct Poet, but *Shakespeare* the greater wit. *Shakespeare* was the *Homer*, or Father of our Dramatick Poets; *Johnon* was the *Virgil*, the pattern of elaborate writing; I admire him, but I love *Shakespeare*.

Dryden: *Of Dramatick Poesie, An Essay*, 1668

I have endeavour'd to represent variety of Humours . . . which was the practice of *Ben Johnson*, whom I think all Dramatick *Poets* ought to imitate, though none are like to come near; he being the only person that appears to me to have made perfect Representations of Human Life: most other Authors that I ever read, either have wild Romantick *Tales*, wherein they strain Love and Honour to that Ridiculous height, that it becomes Burlesque; or in their lower Comedies content themselves with

one or two Humours at most, and those not near so perfect
Characters as the admirable *Johnson* always made, who never
wrote Comedy without seven or eight considerable Humours. I
never saw one except that of *Falstaffe* that was in my judgement
comparable to any of *Johnson*'s considerable Humours; you will
pardon this digression when I tell you he is the man, of all the
World, I most passionately admire for his Excellency in Dram-
matick-Poetry.

Shadwell: Preface to The Sullen Lovers, 1668

Ben Jonson is original; he is, indeed, the only one of the great
dramatists of that day who was not either directly produced, or
very greatly modified, by Shakespeare. In truth, he differs from
our great master in everything — in form and in substance — and
betrays no tokens of his proximity. He is not original in the same
way as Shakespeare is original; but after a fashion of his own,
Ben Jonson is most truly original.

The characters of his plays are, in the strictest sense of the
term, abstractions. Some very prominent feature is taken from
the whole man, and that single feature or humour is made the
basis upon which the entire character is built up. Ben Jonson's
dramatis personae are almost as fixed as the masks of the ancient
actors; you know from the first scene — sometimes from the list
of names — exactly what every one of them is to be. He was a
very accurately observing man; but he cared only to observe
what was external or open to, and likely to impress, the senses.
He individualizes, not so much, if at all, by the exhibition of
moral or intellectual difference, as by the varieties and contrasts
of manners, modes of speech and tricks of temper. . . .

I ought very particularly to call your attention to the extraordinary skill shown by Ben Jonson in contriving situations for
the display of his characters. In fact, his care and anxiety in this
matter led him to do what scarcely any dramatists of that age did
— that is, invent his plots. . . .

Ben Jonson exhibits a sterling English diction, and he has with
great skill contrived varieties of construction; but his style is
rarely sweet or harmonious, in consequence of his labour at
point and strength being so evident. In all his works, in verse and
prose, there is an extraordinary opulence of thought; but it is the
produce of an amassing power in the author and not the growth
from within. Indeed a large proportion of Ben Jonson's thoughts

may be traced to classic or obscure modern writers, by those who are learned and curious enough to follow the steps of this robust, surly, and observing dramatist.

Coleridge: *Literary Remains*, 1836

(*Volpone*) This admirable, indeed, but yet more wonderful than admirable, play is from the fertility and vigour of invention, character, language, and sentiment the strongest proof, how impossible it is to keep up any pleasurable interest in a tale, in which there is no goodness of heart in any of the prominent characters. After the third act, this play becomes not a dead, but a painful, weight on the feelings. . . . Bonario and Celia should have been made in some way or other principals in the plot; which they might have been, and the objects of interest, without having been made characters. . . . If it were possible to lessen the paramountcy of Volpone himself, a most delightful comedy might be produced, by making Celia the ward or niece of Corvino, instead of his wife, and Bonario her lover.

Ibid.

The immediate appeal of Jonson is to the mind; his emotional tone is not in the single verse, but in the design of the whole. But not many people are capable of discovering for themselves the beauty which is only found after labour; and Jonson's industrious readers have been those whose interest was historical and curious, and those who have thought that in discovering the historical and curious interest they have discovered the artistic interest as well. When we say that Jonson requires study, we do not mean study of his classical scholarship or of seventeenth-century manners. We mean intelligent saturation in his work as a whole; we mean that, in order to enjoy him at all, we must get to the centre of his work and his temperament, and that we must see him unbiased by time, as a contemporary. And to see him as a contemporary does not so much require the power of putting ourselves into seventeenth-century London as it requires the power of setting Jonson in our London. . . .

The characters of Shakespeare are such as might exist in different circumstances than those in which Shakespeare sets them. The latter appear to be those which extract from the characters the most intense and interesting realization; but that realization has not exhausted their possibilities. Volpone's life, on the other hand, is bounded by the scene in which it is played; in fact, the life is the life of the scene and is derivatively the life of Volpone; the life of the character is inseparable from the life of the drama. This is not dependence upon a background, or upon a substratum of fact. The emotional effect is single and simple. Whereas in Shakespeare the effect is due to the way in which the characters *act upon* one another, in Jonson it is given by the way the characters *fit in* with each other. The artistic result of *Volpone* is not due to any effect that Volpone, Mosca, Corvino, Corbaccio, Voltore have upon each other, but simply to their combination into a whole. And these figures are not personifications of passions; separately, they have not even that reality, they are constituents. . . . Jonson's characters conform to the logic of the emotions of their world. They are not fancy, because they have a logic of their own; and this logic illuminates the actual world, because it gives us a new point of view from which to inspect it.

A writer of power and intelligence, Jonson endeavoured to promulgate, as a formula and a programme of reform, what he chose to do himself; and he not unnaturally laid down in abstract theory what is in reality a personal point of view. And it is in the end of no value to discuss Jonson's theory and practice unless we recognize and seize this point of view, which escapes the formulae, and which is what makes his plays worth reading. Jonson behaved as the great creative mind that he was: he created his own world, a world from which his followers, as well as the dramatists who were trying to do something wholly different, are excluded. . . . His characters are and remain, like Marlowe's, simplified characters; but the simplification does not consist in the dominance of a particular humour or monomania. That is a very superficial account of it. The simplification consists largely in a reduction of detail, in the seizing of aspects relevant to the relief of an emotional impulse which remains the same for that character, in making the characters conform to a particular setting. This stripping is essential to the art, to which is also essential a flat distortion in the drawing; it is an art of caricature, of great caricature, like Marlowe's. It is a great caricature, which is beautiful; and a great humour, which is serious. The 'world' of Jonson is sufficiently large; it is a world of poetic imagination; it is sombre. . . .

If we approach Jonson with less frozen awe of his learning,

with a clearer understanding of his 'rhetoric' and its applications, if we grasp the fact that the knowledge required of the reader is not archaeology, but knowledge of Jonson, we can derive not only instruction in two-dimensional life — but enjoyment. We can even apply him, be aware of him as a part of our literary inheritance craving further expression. Of all the dramatists of his time, Jonson is probably the one whom the present age would find the most sympathetic, if it knew him. There is a brutality, a lack of sentiment, a polished surface, a handling of large bold designs in brilliant colours, which ought to attract about three thousand people in London and elsewhere. At least, if we had a contemporary Shakespeare and a contemporary Jonson, it might be the Jonson who would arouse the enthusiasm of the intelligentsia.

T. S. Eliot: *Selected Essays*, 1932

Bibliography

Ben Jonson: Works, edited by C. H. Herford, P. and E. M. Simpson. Oxford (1925–52).
    This is the definitive edition of Jonson's works. The first two volumes contain a general introduction and essays on the separate plays; the last three contain commentary and notes.

A Study of Ben Jonson, by A. C. Swinburne (1889).
    Rather 'old-fashioned', but still a very perceptive book.

Ben Jonson, by G. G. Smith (1919).
    In the *English Men of Letters* series; critical biography.

Ben Jonson of Westminster, by M. Chute (1953).
    Life only; very readable.

Drama and Society in the Age of Jonson, by L. C. Knights (1937).
    A brilliant relation of Jonson to the social and economic background of his age.

The Broken Compass, by E. B. Partridge (1958).
    A modern critical study of Jonson's poetry.